*Dignity Endures*

# THE AZRIELI SERIES OF HOLOCAUST SURVIVOR MEMOIRS: PUBLISHED TITLES

# Dignity Endures

*Judith Rubinstein*

THE AZRIELI FOUNDATION
www.azrielifoundation.org

Cover and book design by Mark Goldstein
Endpaper maps by Martin Gilbert
Map on page xxxiii by François Blanc

LIBRARY AND ARCHIVES CANADA CATALOGUING IN PUBLICATION

Rubinstein, Judith, 1920–2013, author
    Dignity Endures/ Judith Rubinstein.

(Azrieli series of Holocaust survivor memoirs. Series IX)
Includes index.
ISBN 978-1-988065-25-0 (softcover) · 8 7 6 5 4 3 2 1

1. Rubinstein, Judith, 1920–2013. 2. Jews — Hungary — Biography. 3. Holocaust, Jewish (1939–1945) — Poland — Personal narratives. 4. Holocaust, Jewish (1939–1945) — Germany — Personal narratives. 5. Auschwitz (Concentration camp). 6. Malchow (Concentration camp). 7. Holocaust survivors — Italy — Biography. 8. Holocaust survivors — Canada — Biography. 9. Autobiographies — I. Azrieli Foundation, issuing body II. Title. III. Series: Azrieli series of Holocaust survivor memoirs. Series IX

DS135.H93R83 2018        940.53'18092        C2018-900631-5

PRINTED IN CANADA

# The Azrieli Series of Holocaust Survivor Memoirs

Naomi Azrieli, Publisher

Jody Spiegel, Program Director
Arielle Berger, Managing Editor
Matt Carrington, Editor
Elizabeth Lasserre, Senior Editor, French-Language Editions
Elin Beaumont, Senior Education Outreach and Program Facilitator
Catherine Person, Educational Outreach and Events Coordinator,
   Quebec and French Canada
Stephanie Corazza, Education and Curriculum Associate
Marc-Olivier Cloutier, Educational Outreach and Events Assistant,
   Quebec and French Canada
Elizabeth Banks, Digital Asset Curator and Archivist
Susan Roitman, Office Manager (Toronto)
Mary Mellas, Executive Assistant and Human Resources (Montreal)

Mark Goldstein, Art Director
François Blanc, Cartographer
Bruno Paradis, Layout, French-Language Editions

# Contents

# Series Preface:
# In their own words. . .

*In telling these stories, the writers have liberated themselves. For so many years we did not speak about it, even when we became free people living in a free society. Now, when at last we are writing about what happened to us in this dark period of history, knowing that our stories will be read and live on, it is possible for us to feel truly free. These unique historical documents put a face on what was lost, and allow readers to grasp the enormity of what happened to six million Jews — one story at a time.*

David J. Azrieli, C.M., C.Q., M.Arch
Holocaust survivor and founder, The Azrieli Foundation

Since the end of World War II, approximately 40,000 Jewish Holocaust survivors have immigrated to Canada. Who they are, where they came from, what they experienced and how they built new lives for themselves and their families are important parts of our Canadian heritage. The Azrieli Foundation's Holocaust Survivor Memoirs Program was established in 2005 to preserve and share the memoirs written by those who survived the twentieth-century Nazi genocide of the Jews of Europe and later made their way to Canada. The program is guided by the conviction that each survivor of the Holocaust has a remarkable story to tell, and that such stories play an important role in education about tolerance and diversity.

Millions of individual stories are lost to us forever. By preserving the stories written by survivors and making them widely available to a broad audience, the Azrieli Foundation's Holocaust Survivor Memoirs Program seeks to sustain the memory of all those who perished at the hands of hatred, abetted by indifference and apathy. The personal accounts of those who survived against all odds are as different as the people who wrote them, but all demonstrate the courage, strength, wit and luck that it took to prevail and survive in such terrible adversity. The memoirs are also moving tributes to people — strangers and friends — who risked their lives to help others, and who, through acts of kindness and decency in the darkest of moments, frequently helped the persecuted maintain faith in humanity and courage to endure. These accounts offer inspiration to all, as does the survivors' desire to share their experiences so that new generations can learn from them.

The Holocaust Survivor Memoirs Program collects, archives and publishes select survivor memoirs and makes the print editions available free of charge to educational institutions and Holocaust-education programs across Canada. They are also available for sale to the general public at bookstores. All revenues to the Azrieli Foundation from the sales of the Azrieli Series of Holocaust Survivor Memoirs go toward the publishing and educational work of the memoirs program.

~

The Azrieli Foundation would like to express appreciation to the following people for their invaluable efforts in producing this book: Doris Bergen, Sherry Dodson (Maracle Inc), Barbara Kamieński, Therese Parent, and Margie Wolfe & Emma Rodgers of Second Story Press.

# About the Glossary

The following memoir contains a number of terms, concepts and historical references that may be unfamiliar to the reader. For information on major organizations; significant historical events and people; geographical locations; religious and cultural terms; and foreign-language words and expressions that will help give context and background to the events described in the text, please see the glossary beginning on page 113.

# About the Cover

My mother, Rochelle Rubinstein, created the artwork on the cover of my grandmother Judith Rubinstein's memoir, *Dignity Endures*. The cover combines two images: a woodblock print of a woman nursing a baby printed over a family photograph of my mother's great-uncle and great-aunt Heszu and Rozsi Hofstadter, cousin Tom and herself as a child, wearing a red coat and hat sewn by Judith. The nursing woman symbolizes the intensity of motherhood and the family bond. The image of the nursing woman also represents my extraordinary grandmother. Her expression contains a complexity of emotions: pride, devotion and triumph, as well as anguish at the unspeakable losses that preceded this moment (she gave birth to her first child in a DP camp in 1948). There is also a touch of defiance in her expression, saying, *Hitler, you didn't win — I'm here, creating a life*. It was crucial to my grandmother to pass on her story, to honour the past, but also to embrace the present and be hopeful about the future.

When my grandmother left this world, at peace and with the greatest possible dignity, she left us with a model for how to live with grace, with respect for all people and with a love of life. Judith's children, grandchildren and great-grandchildren, and everyone who knew her, drank it all in.

*Alisha Kaplan*, granddaughter of Judith Rubinstein

# Introduction

It was only years after her liberation, when she was no longer consumed by the daily struggle to stay alive, that my dear mother, Judith Rubinstein, was free to ponder the catastrophe that had befallen her family and her people. Recalling the past had a cathartic and healing effect for my mother, enabling her to find meaning in what would otherwise have been unbearably meaningless. But Judith was the exception to the rule among many Holocaust survivors.

Far more characteristic of survivors was my dear father Bill (Béla) Rubinstein, who never talked about the past. Whenever a conversation turned toward the period before his arrival in Canada, he would try his best to change the subject. If this proved ineffective, he would find an excuse to leave the room.

Like many survivors, Judith seethed with bitterness and despair in the years following the Holocaust. At the first *Yizkor* memorial service she attended after the war, Judith simply could not bring herself to recite the words of the prayer, much as she yearned to honour the memory of her murdered parents and brothers.

Her initial impulse was to flee from the Jewish identity that had brought her so much anguish. In time, however, she came to realize that severing her roots brought no satisfaction, only dismal emptiness. Judith found it in her heart to begin participating in *Yizkor* services, and she returned to the traditional Jewish teaching that *zakhor*, the obligation to remember, needs to be coupled with *shamor*, the loving observance of the heritage of our ancestors and its transmission in turn to our descendants. Throughout the long, turbulent history of the Jewish people, these traditions have infused our lives with purpose and given us the strength to carry on.

Judith's stories about her earlier life gestated within her for a long time. During her first years in Canada, the memories were an achingly solitary affair. The tragic and horrifying experiences of European Jews stood as a yawning chasm between those Jews who had been fortunate to come to Toronto before the war and the survivors who joined them afterward.

Not long after Judith's arrival in Toronto in September 1948, a curious neighbour asked the newcomer what had brought her to Canada. Judith responded matter-of-factly that almost her entire family had been murdered by the Germans during the war. She herself managed to survive Auschwitz and her husband-to-be survived Hungarian forced labour camps. She added that she and her husband could not have simply returned home as if nothing had happened. At the time no country in the world wanted to take in Jewish refugees, so they languished for almost three years in an Italian refugee camp, until finally Canada was the first country to open the door.

A long, awkward silence was followed by a deep sigh and a plaintive lament: "*Oy*, Mrs. Rubinstein, you can't imagine how hard it was in Toronto during the Great Depression. We didn't even have butter to put on our poor children's bread!"

At a loss for words, Judith brought the conversation to an abrupt conclusion. How could her neighbour comprehend horrors utterly beyond the realm of her experience? She decided that it would be prudent to keep her memories to herself.

Almost two decades would pass before Judith opened up about what came to be known as the Holocaust or Shoah, perceiving that people were finally becoming receptive to these stories. Beginning in the early 1960s, extensive media coverage of the Eichmann trial and the publication of works like Elie Wiesel's *Night* chipped away at the barriers separating survivors from non-survivors.

So it was that an immigrant to Canada who had never had the opportunity to learn English properly decided years later to enroll in a creative writing course. Judith was determined to acquire the tools she needed to tell her story. Younger family members tried teaching her how to create and edit documents on a computer, but she just could not master the necessary hand–eye coordination. She continued to labour away by hand in a hard-to-decipher script, the consequence of a left-handed young girl being compelled long ago to write with her right hand.

Sometime after she started writing, this elderly woman who had never addressed an audience before became a popular speaker at the Neuberger Holocaust Education Centre in Toronto. Judith derived special satisfaction from engaging with schoolchildren, to whom the future belonged, both non-Jews and Jews, thousands of them over the years.

It was precisely the prosaic nature of Judith's stories about ordinary people living commonplace lives that was so arresting: the underlying message was that her family, friends and neighbours were selected to be killed in the gas chambers not because of anything they had done, but for one reason only — they were unfortunate enough to have been born Jewish at the wrong time and in the wrong place.

As part of her presentations, Judith would gesture toward the blue number on her forearm and explain that this tattoo was how the Nazis tagged Jewish prisoners kept alive for slave labour at death camps like Auschwitz-Birkenau. These marks were not just an efficient German administrative procedure, akin to ranchers branding their cattle to keep track of them: the numbers were a deliberate attempt to dehumanize the Jews. By replacing the prisoners' names with numbers, the Germans were trying to extinguish their souls before murdering their bodies.

I have always been in awe of my parents and their circle of fellow survivors among whom I was privileged to grow up. By remaining decent, affable, highly engaged human beings, these survivors triumphed gloriously over the evil people who had tried so hard to degrade them and to destroy their lives. Remarkably, after all they had endured, these survivors were able to muster the courage to get married and bring Jewish children into the world. They worked hard to support their families, hoping that in this wonderful new land, their children would be blessed with lives far better than their own had been. Many survivors have achieved outstanding success in Canada and have contributed munificently to their communities and to society at large.

I am proud to be the child of two such people.

~

*The hand of fate shall also seize Hungarian Jewry. And the later this occurs, and the stronger this Jewry becomes, the more cruel and hard shall be the blow, which shall be delivered with greater savagery. There is no escape.*

*Theodore Herzl*, letter to a friend, March 10, 1903

The Budapest-born father of political Zionism had a remarkable ability to foresee what others could or would not. During the Hungarian "Golden Era" of the latter nineteenth and early twentieth centuries, the Jews of Hungary enjoyed a period of unprecedented social advancement and economic prosperity. Euphoric at their good fortune, they expressed their gratitude through fervent patriotism and adoration of all things Hungarian. It took a disenchanted visionary like Herzl to see the disturbing signs pointing to a tragic denouement.

So resolute was the Jews' love for Hungary that as late as spring 1944, when millions of Jews in neighbouring countries had already been murdered, amid ever-intensifying antisemitism at home, "Magyars of the Israelite faith" (as Hungarian Jews liked to describe themselves) were still in denial that such a thing could ever happen in their beloved Fatherland.

When Winston Churchill learned how quickly and barbarously the Jews of Hungary had been destroyed by the Germans and their ardent Hungarian collaborators, he remarked that this was "probably the greatest and most horrible crime ever committed in the history of the world." How could everything have gone so dreadfully wrong for Jews in Hungary after such an auspicious period of integration? And how could the Hungarian Jews have been so oblivious to the catastrophe unfolding before their eyes?

As the son of parents who had their former lives destroyed forever by the Shoah in Hungary, I have long struggled with these questions. The answers, I believe, lie in an understanding of the unique history of Jewish-Hungarian relations.

Jews were present in the Carpathian Basin at least six hundred years before the Hungarians. In the days of the Roman Empire, Jewish traders and slaves were already living in and travelling through the remote provinces then known as Pannonia and Dacia.

The savage Magyar horsemen came storming into the region from the steppes of central Asia in the ninth and tenth centuries. As pagans, the Magyars did not regard Jews differently at first than any of the other strangers they encountered in their new surroundings. After their conversion to Christianity, however, they came to adopt characteristic anti-Jewish attitudes. Consequently, throughout the Middle Ages, periods of relative peace and prosperity for the Jews of Hungary alternated with periods of religiously and economically inspired turmoil and persecution, as was generally the pattern in Christian Europe.

Most of Hungary fell under Austrian rule in the early eighteenth century, marking the beginning of the modern period for Hungarian Jewry. A large wave of immigrants, primarily from Moravia but also from Poland, soon far outnumbered the native Jewish population. These people consisted mainly of village-dwelling peddlers and tradesmen. Initially, the Austrians were not favourably disposed toward the Jews, subjecting them to economic and judicial restrictions and punitive taxes. However, as the spirit of reform took root, these measures were eventually eliminated.

The great turning point for Hungarian Jews came in 1867, when the dual monarchy of Austria-Hungary was established and the Hungarian aristocratic class headed by King Charles IV assumed the governance of Hungary. The vast territory now under their control posed a vexing challenge: although Hungary's historic heartland was populated almost exclusively by ethnic Magyars, the peripheral areas encompassed large numbers of Czechs, Slovaks, Romanians, Croats and others harbouring nationalistic aspirations of their own. But there were also over half a million Jews spread throughout the country, their numbers growing rapidly through a combination of immigration and a high birth rate. At the time, the mostly town-dwelling Jews in Hungary spoke either German or Yiddish, since Hungarian was the language of the peasants. Intent on increasing the number of "Magyars" in the realm in order to consolidate their hold on the periphery, the rulers made an unusual proposal to the Jews: if the Jews agreed to adopt the Hungarian language and culture as their own and pledge undivided loyalty to the state, they would be granted the same rights of citizenship as Christians. The Jewish community accepted the proposal with alacrity, and a bill granting them full emancipation was passed by parliament.

The Jews of Hungary took full advantage of the new and unprecedented opportunities. Freed of long-standing constraints in a newly meritocratic society, they were accepted into the universities in large numbers, and for the first time, they were able to enter the professions. Although Jews constituted no more than 5 per cent of the population, in very short order 60 per cent of the medical doctors, 50 per cent of the lawyers, 42 per cent of the journalists and 26 per cent of those engaged in literature and the arts were Jewish. In addition, Jews played a very prominent role in the transition from a feudal agrarian economy to a modern capitalistic one. They were disproportionately represented in banking and finance, providing much of the funding for new industrial enterprises, some of the largest of which were Jewish-owned. Previously barred from acquiring property, Jews also became heavily involved in the ownership and administration of agricultural estates and the marketing of produce, and 60 per cent of all the merchants in the country were Jewish.

Deeply appreciative of the dramatic improvement in their status, Hungarian Jews often became "more Magyar than the Magyars." However, their new-found infatuation was not reciprocated. Many Jews who rose to the pinnacle of success yearned to join the aristocratic class but were snubbed by the high-born who regarded nobility as a function of heredity, not attainment. The displacement of the old feudal order by a modern meritocracy provoked particular enmity among those who saw their inherited privileges suddenly usurped by Jewish upstarts. At the other end of the social scale, the large peasant majority came to resent the Jews who controlled the estates on which they worked and the stores in which they shopped, seeing them as economic exploiters. No less resentful were the many peasants flocking to the towns to work in new Jewish-owned industrial enterprises. At the same time, as an unintended consequence of their Magyar patriotism, Hungarian Jews managed to antagonize the other ethnic minorities in Hungary striving to assert their own national identities. And when Judaism was granted equal legal status with Catholicism and Protestantism in 1895, this provoked strident opposition, particularly from the Roman Catholic Church.

In short, the spectacular advancement of the Jews facilitated by their emancipation turned virtually everyone in the country against them. The following years saw a great increase in anti-Jewish propaganda, and political antisemitism became a force in the Hungarian parliament. The Tiszaeszlár blood libel of 1882, a throwback to the Dark Ages in which Hungarian Jews were falsely accused of murdering Christian children as part of a Jewish ritual, engendered many violent outbursts against Jews.

Nevertheless, the rulers of Hungary persisted in protecting the Jews for two pragmatic reasons. First, the country benefitted greatly from their enormous contributions in many fields. Second, the fast-growing Hungarian-speaking Jewish population still provided a strategic counterbalance to the other minorities in Hungary. For their part, the Jews continued to have faith in their royal patrons, despite the widespread animosity directed against them.

The Hungarian-Jewish accord eventually broke down following World War I. Under the terms of the Treaty of Trianon in 1920, the vanquished Austro-Hungarian Empire was dismantled, with Austria and Hungary emerging as separate countries. Hungary was dealt an exceptionally harsh blow, losing two-thirds of its territory, which was assigned to the newly created states of Czechoslovakia, Romania and Yugoslavia. Half the total population of the former Hungarian monarchy, including a third of all ethnic Magyars, was now isolated on the other side of international borders. Added to this was the loss of Hungary's seaports, much of its industry, railways and other infrastructure, as well as up to 90 per cent of its considerable natural resources. A national trauma rooted in a sense of profound grievance against a historic injustice gripped the Hungarian nation.

The value of the Jews in bolstering the demographic standing of the Magyars was nullified, since the shrunken new Hungary was homogeneously Hungarian. The short-lived communist revolution following the war, with its prominent Jewish leadership, further fanned the antisemitic flames. Jews could now be hated, paradoxically, both for being capitalists and for being communists.

Subsequent national leaders, realizing that Jewish contributions were more essential than ever in the much-diminished Hungarian economy, cynically continued to reassure the Jews that their status was secure. Many Jews continued to believe them, but by now, the downward spiral for Hungarian Jews was inexorable.

Ominously, in 1920 the Numerus Clausus Act was passed, limiting university admissions of Jews to 5 per cent, their presumed percentage of the population. The inevitable consequence was a precipitous drop in standards, to the detriment of the Hungarian public. For example, in the field of medicine, Hungary plummeted from excellence to mediocrity as highly qualified Jewish medical school applicants were forced to leave the country. My father's cousin, Dr. Ernő Sebők, who studied in Italy and ended up in the United States, was one of many who left. In their rage against the perfidy of Trianon, Hungarians failed to grasp that by scapegoating the Jews they were actually causing themselves severe harm.

Soon after the Nazis came to power in Germany in 1933, Hungary formed a political and military alliance with Germany, and eventually Germany helped Hungary regain much of its lost territory. The beholden government of Regent Miklós Horthy, a self-professed antisemite, passed a series of measures modelled on Nazi Germany's Nuremberg Laws. The First Jewish Law of 1938 limited the participation of Jews in a wide range of professional and commercial fields to 20 per cent. The Second Jewish Law of 1939 further reduced this limit to 5 per cent and also barred Jews from government jobs. In addition, Jews were no longer permitted to own businesses, employ Christians in their homes or maintain social relations with Christians. Severe constraints were also imposed on the political rights of Jews. Following the racist lead of Nazi Germany, the Third Jewish Law of 1941 prohibited intermarriage between Jews and Christians and extended all these restrictions to about 100,000 Christians who were defined as Jewish for having at least two Jewish grandparents.

The Hungarian Jewish leaders continued to urge patience. They had convinced themselves that the ever-expanding discriminatory legislation was the government's shrewd strategy to protect the Jews against the far more drastic demands of its Nazi partners. They took it as a positive sign that Regent Horthy steadfastly refused Hitler's demand to deport the Jews of Hungary, beyond the 20,000 or so who were not Hungarian citizens (mostly Polish and Russian). They also chose to dismiss as an anomaly the massacres of most of these people by the German SS and Einsatzgruppen and Hungarian gendarmes at the Ukrainian city of Kamenets-Podolsk on August 27 and 28, 1941, and in Novi Sad, Yugoslavia (now Serbia), in 1942.

~

The Jewish community of Szerencs, the northeastern town in Hungary where Judith grew up, came into being at the beginning of the nineteenth century and was well established when Judith moved there. Besides the Orthodox synagogue to be expected in this conservative region of the country, Szerencs boasted a Jewish free loan fund (providing interest-free loans for those in need), a burial society and a small yeshiva. In the early years, most of the Jews in Szerencs were wine merchants. Later on, when the town became a major railroad hub, a sugar factory — the largest in Europe at the time — was established there, followed by a nationally renowned chocolate factory. An ever-growing number of Jews moved to Szerencs, attracted by its commercial prospects. As elsewhere in Hungary, the Jews formed most of the mercantile class in Szerencs, bringing significant material benefits to the general population but simultaneously generating socio-economic tensions.

In July 1918, as the Austro-Hungarian Empire lurched toward ignominious defeat in World War I, a wave of antisemitism was unleashed in Szerencs, as it was in many other places, by embittered citizens in need of someone to blame. Local Jews were arrested on trumped-up charges, and large amounts of merchandise and cash belonging to members of the Szerencs Jewish community were confiscated.

Judith Schwarcz was six years old in 1926 when her family moved to Szerencs from the smaller town of Mezőcsát. The Jews whom Judith and her family encountered in Szerencs were, like themselves, mostly of Galician origin. Both of Judith's maternal grandparents, Aryeh Leib and Feige Leah Hofstadter, as well as her paternal grandmother, Judith Schwarcz, hailed from Dukla (now in Poland), and her paternal grandfather, Eliezer Menachem Mendel Schwarcz, was a native of Zalozce (now part of Ukraine).

During the period between the establishment of the Dual Monarchy in 1867 and its dismemberment in 1920, the province of Galicia was a primitive backwater of the empire. Many of the poor and oppressed Jews in the region took advantage of the opportunity to cross the open frontier into Hungary, hoping to benefit from that country's vigorous economy and progressive civil rights. They settled mostly in small towns in the north-east, such as Mezőcsát, Szerencs and Mezőkövesd, home of the Hofstadters. The Galician Jews found the traditional small-town religiosity of the Jews already inhabiting these places far more congenial than the modern secularity of larger centres. In post-Trianon Hungary, 65 per cent of Jews, who lived largely in the greater Budapest area, identified with the moderately reformist Neolog movement. A mere 5 per cent belonged to the traditionalist Status Quo Ante group. The remaining 30 per cent were Orthodox, adhering to the old Ashkenazic rituals and liturgy championed by the charismatic nineteenth-century anti-reform firebrand Rabbi Moshe Sofer. The Galician newcomers blended comfortably into the existing Orthodox communities, mostly leaving behind the Hasidic-influenced rituals and liturgy they had known in the old country. After 1920, the dynamic Hungarian Hasidic dynasties such as Szatmár and Munkács were stranded in the newly-created states of Romania and Czechoslovakia, and their influence in what was left of Hungary was greatly diminished.

The Yiddish-speaking members of the first generation who moved to these small Hungarian towns were unable to master the Hungarian language and culture. However, by the second generation, that of my grandparents, Hungarian became the beloved native tongue, and Yiddish was abandoned. No scion of fierce Magyar equestrians was more devoted to the Fatherland than these children of Polish Jewish immigrants, thankful to be living in what was, in their minds, the best country in the world.

Judith's father, Elias Schwarcz, had a low-paying but respectable job as a public high school teacher, supplemented by a government stipend for his services as secretary of the Szerencs Jewish community. In 1939, he was dismissed from both positions under the Second Jewish Law and, like everyone else in the community, struggled to support his family.

Judith was a good student with a thirst for knowledge. She was devastated when, along with all other school-aged Jews, she was barred from continuing her formal education. Throughout the rest of her life, she tried her best to compensate by being a voracious reader and an attentive listener.

Having been drawn into World War II and the conflict with the Soviet Union by its treaty with Nazi Germany, the Hungarian government watched with alarm as its army was decimated on the eastern front. On March 19, 1944, the Germans seized direct control of Hungary to prevent it from capitulating to the Allied side. Adolf Eichmann arrived in Budapest two days later with a clear mandate to resolve the "Jewish Question." He brought with him a mere two hundred Germans, including guards and typists, knowing that he could count on large numbers of eager Hungarian collaborators to carry out the dirty work.

On April 7, 1944, two Slovakian inmates of Auschwitz-Birkenau, Rudolph Vrba and Alfred Wetzler, escaped — not at all a simple feat. Having witnessed the extensive preparations being made in the death camp in anticipation of the arrival of hundreds of thousands of Hungarian Jews, they desperately wanted to deliver a warning to their brethren. They managed to reach Slovakia and fully briefed the members of the Jewish Council, who in turn passed on the information to the official leadership of the Hungarian Jewish community in Budapest.

Tragically, it was far too late for the shocking information to make a difference.

On April 16, the local police rounded up the 916 Jews of Szerencs. Among them were Judith Schwarcz, her parents and her younger brothers. They were first assembled in the synagogue and communal buildings, where they had their remaining possessions stolen from them. At the beginning of June, the Jews of Szerencs and those of the surrounding settlements, a total of almost 2,000 people, were moved to the ghetto in the nearby town of Miskolc.

On June 14 and 15, Jews in the ghetto were crammed into cattle cars without adequate food, water, fresh air or sanitary facilities. The Nazis told them that they were being sent by train to Germany to assist the war effort by working in a munitions factory, a story they accepted, just as they had accepted the many assurances of successive Hungarian governments and of their own communal leaders that everything would be fine. Upon disembarking from the train, these Hungarian Jews learned that their destination had not been Germany, but instead a town in Poland by the name of Oświęcim, or as the Germans called it, Auschwitz.

By working hard and remaining useful to the Nazis, as well as benefitting from a good amount of luck, Judith was among the few Jews of Szerencs to survive what Elie Wiesel later called "the kingdom of night." Her parents and young brothers never stood a chance.

Out of a total of about 825,000 Jews in Hungary, some 565,000 were murdered and 260,000 survived.

After the war, Judith married Béla Rubinstein of Szentistván, a neighbour of her mother's family in Mezőkövesd. Had the war not disrupted their lives, the two of them never would have crossed paths. Béla had been happily married with two young sons when he was drafted into forced labour by the Hungarian regime, along with many other able-bodied Jewish men. In a terrible twist of fate, while he was thus compelled to be far from home, his family was deported to Auschwitz, never to return. Béla was twelve years older than Judith. It was very common for older Jewish men like my father who had lost their families in the Holocaust to marry younger women like my mother who had been prevented by the wartime madness from getting married earlier.

∼

At the end of her life, Judith Rubinstein expressed serenity in the face of death. To all who asked how she was feeling, she would respond simply: "My bags are packed." As a young woman emerging from the inferno of the Holocaust at the age of twenty-four, astonished that she was still alive, Judith could not have imagined that she would reach the venerable age of ninety-two, living what was on balance a very good life. For my mother, every single day after liberation was a wondrous gift, but it had been enough and she had no regrets. She left us on the ninth day of Shvat, 5773, January 19, 2013.

The number of living survivors is dwindling, and in a short while they will all be gone. We who remain behind must prepare for a world in which there are no living witnesses to the calamitous destruction of European Jewry. We have been spoiled all these years by having in our midst remarkable people like Judith Rubinstein. Not only did they testify to the horrors of the past with their tattooed forearms and powerful words, but in their triumphant struggle to rebuild broken lives, they also affirmed their faith in the redeemability of a deeply flawed humanity. By doing so, they gave us hope for the future.

Who now will bear witness?

Who will guide us?

Inspire us?

Comfort us?

We shall have to devise new ways, inevitably less direct, to continue this sacred duty. Let us pray that we are up to the challenge. The Azrieli Foundation's Series of Holocaust Survivor Memoirs, of which the present volume is the latest offering, will be one way to keep the memories alive and ever-present.

*Robert Eli Rubinstein*
Author of *An Italian Renaissance: Choosing Life in Canada* and son of Judith Rubinstein
2018

SOURCES

Braham, Randolph L., ed. *The Geographical Encyclopedia of the Holocaust in Hungary.* Evanston: Northwestern University Press, 2013.

Braham, Randolph L., ed. *Hungarian-Jewish Studies.* New York: World Federation of Hungarian Jews, 1966.

Braham, Randolph L., and Béla Vágó, eds. *The Holocaust in Hungary: Forty Years Later.* New York: Social Science Monographs and Institute for Holocaust Studies, CUNY, 1985.

Hertz, Isaac, director. Interview of Judith Rubinstein. Life Is Strange. Video Documentary. 2012. https://vimeo.com/60870455

Katzburg, Nathaniel. "Hungary." In *Encyclopaedia Judaica.* 8:1088–1108. Jerusalem: Keter Publishing, 1972.

Mandelbaum, Mordechai, ed. *Hofstedter Family Chronicles.* Toronto: Private Publication, 1992.

Patai, Raphael. *The Jews of Hungary: History, Culture, Psychology.* Detroit: Wayne State University Press, 1996.

Rubinstein, Judith. USC Shoah Foundation, Visual History Archive video, January 31, 1995. http://vhaonline.usc.edu/viewingPage?testimonyID=713&returnIndex=0

Rubinstein, Robert Eli. *An Italian Renaissance: Choosing Life in Canada.* New York: Urim Publications, 2010.

Rubinstein, Robert Eli. "Making Amends." *Mosaic,* April 27, 2014. https://mosaic-magazine.com/observation/2014/04/making-amends/

Rubinstein, Robert Eli. "Who Now Will Bear Witness?" *The Times of Israel.* April 12, 2015. http://blogs.timesofisrael.com/who-now-will-bear-witness/

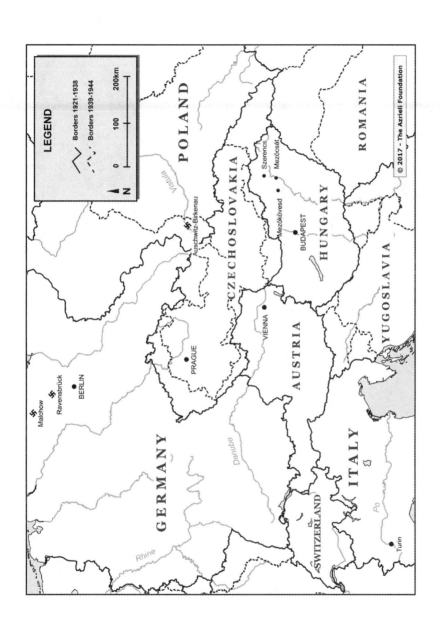

**LEGEND**

Borders 1921-1938
Borders 1939-1944

0    100    200km

N

POLAND

GERMANY

Malchow
Ravensbrück
BERLIN

Rhine

Vistula

Auschwitz-Birkenau

CZECHOSLOVAKIA

PRAGUE

Szerencs
Mezőcsát

Mezőkövesd

BUDAPEST

HUNGARY

ROMANIA

VIENNA

AUSTRIA

Danube

SWITZERLAND

ITALY

Po

Turin

YUGOSLAVIA

© 2017 - The Azrieli Foundation

*I am alive today thanks to my mother's intervention in saving my life from the gas chamber in Auschwitz-Birkenau. I am forever grateful for the gift of life she gave me. The pain of losing her so young will never leave me. May her memory be a blessing.*

# Bittersweet Memories

My parents, Elias Schwarcz and Rachel Hofstadter, were married near the end of World War I. Soon afterwards, my father leased the only hotel in their sleepy, mid-sized town of Mezőcsát, Hungary, and brought his young bride into the hectic business of managing a hotel. The hotel's rooms were always full of visiting dignitaries and travelling salesmen, and the banquet hall was used for every official function, including election victories, banquets, sports events and visiting theatre groups. Mother ran the kitchen very efficiently with only a few helpers and supplied the dining room with wholesome food and delicacies.

On the night in September 19, 1920, when I decided to make my entry into the world, a huge ball was in progress at the hotel honouring the winning football crew from our town. My parents' bedroom was on the second floor, just under the stomping feet of the dancers in the ballroom on the third floor. As the Roma musicians blared all night, a midwife attended Mother through her labour pains and my birth. No wonder I love music so much, especially the melodies of the Roma people. Two years later, my brother Yitzhak was born in the same room.

Since my brother and I were underfoot a lot as children, our parents realized that a hotel was not a good place to raise a family. Father decided to return to his real love, teaching, for which he was well qualified. He accepted a position teaching religion in the public high school in Szerencs, a medium-sized town close to the Czechoslovakian border, and also became the secretary of the Jewish community there.

I was six in 1926 when we moved to Szerencs and settled into the rented house that would be our new home. We had friendly neighbours, and it wasn't long before Father was well known and highly respected by Jews and gentiles alike for his knowledge and gentle manners. But for me it was a difficult transition. I had had to give up the familiar surroundings that I had always known and the large, loving and caring family of which I was used to being a part, as my paternal grandparents and many uncles, aunts and cousins from my father's side of the family lived in Mezőcsát.

Szerencs means "luck" in Hungarian. According to folklore, Árpád, the first leader of the Hungarian tribe from the family of Huns, charged down from the Carpathian Mountains with his nomads and occupied the land that had previously belonged to different tribes and made it into a homestead for the Hungarian nation. "This place will bring luck to us," Árpád apparently said to his comrades upon descending to the site of our home town. And the name stuck. When we lived there, the population of Szerencs was made up of people from a mixture of different backgrounds and religions, all living in harmony.

The town was built on the side of a rocky mountain, which towered over us like a giant, and from our windows we could see the majestic rock formations of different shapes and sizes. My family had previously lived in an area of flat land, and I had never seen a mountain. I was a real dreamer, and the mountain became my best friend and my consolation for the lack of company. The mountain was always there for me. I spent all of my free time picking its violets and other pretty flowers and sitting in the tall grass listening to the sound of singing birds and chirping insects. I loved rolling down the gentle slopes, my nose full of the smell of the fresh grass. While I was with my mountain, I forgot the world around me and was happy.

The thick forests on the mountain were ever changing but always beautiful. In the early spring when the sun shone on the rocks, especially after a heavy rain, the wet rocks seemed to change colour to a beautiful pine hue, and I was fascinated by this beautiful sight. All the cemeteries were on one side of the mountain, and we often went to visit them since we knew most of the people who were buried there. One large mausoleum, a prominent family's burial place, was our favourite spot. There were low benches at the front of the building, and we loved to sit there listening to the silence and breathing in the special scent of the cypress trees and the very pleasant smell of the climbing roses.

There were caves in the mountains where the younger generation would play, and after I made some friends we loved to play hide-and-seek in them. It was cool and dark inside the caves. They gave us an eerie feeling, and we loved to pretend that we were in danger inside them, even though we knew very well that we could get out easily if we wanted to. There were also huge wine cellars under the mountains since the whole region was grape-growing country.

When that first summer was over, though, the harsh reality woke me from my dreaming state: I had to go to school. Since there was no nursery school or kindergarten in Hungary, my first encounter with the school system started with Grade 1. School felt like torture to me when I first started. I felt very lonely, and the other children never bothered to talk to me. It was difficult to make friends, especially since I was shy. Then, when I had been in school for only a few weeks, I became very sick with whooping cough, and the doctor recommended a change of climate — the only treatment available at the time for that disease.

Father travelled with me back to our old hometown of Mezőcsát and left me there in my paternal grandparents' care. But my excitement at being back home again was short-lived because the doctor told the family to stay away from me or they too might catch the dreaded disease. I spent the next six months in solitary confinement with nobody to play with. Grandma was too busy with the household chores to entertain me, and only Grandpa took pity on me by playing checkers in the evenings with a very unhappy little girl.

When the doctor finally let me go home to my parents, I had missed so much school work that I had to wait another year to start Grade 1 again. But, through sheer determination, I worked hard to catch up and did well. Being a good student helped to build my self-confidence, and from that time on I was rarely unhappy. By the end of the year, I had become part of a happy gang of lively little girls.

I met Sári Selymes in Grade 1, and she became my best friend. Sári was one of six children in a fun-loving and easygoing family. She was tall and very slim with blond curly hair, blue eyes and dimples on her cheeks. She also had a musical voice. As the first-born, she took her role in her family very seriously and expected her younger sisters to follow her example and listen to her authority. When they disobeyed her wishes, she was prone to the occasional tantrum. Sári had some special privileges as the oldest of her siblings and became accustomed to having her own way most of the time.

Because of our different temperaments, we got along very well. Usually, I was the follower. I admired Sári's daring and outgoing personality and she respected my better school performance. On weekends, Sári's house was the meeting place for all the children of our neighbourhood. Her mother, whom we called Aunt Elizabeth, was a hefty, jovial person who always seemed in good humour and tolerated our presence. We had a lot of fun in their house. In the summertime, while Aunt Elizabeth had her daily siesta, she let us rummage through her closet and we excitedly played dress-up. She was our best audience, listening to our improvised performances, dancing, singing and reciting poetry. After we finished our routine, she rewarded us with a delicious afternoon snack.

We had the same teacher for all six grades, and school, which took up six days a week, was strict and demanding. The teachers assigned a lot of homework and punishment was doled out readily for the slightest misbehaviour. Being forced to stand in the corner for a long time or to kneel on bricks were common ways that disobedient children were punished. Hitting children's hands with a stick was also an accepted form of discipline. If the teacher didn't like someone, it was just that child's bad luck to have to endure these punishments.

My teacher, Mrs. Hormach, was a middle-aged widow. When I started in her class in Grade 1, I was a shy little girl, and Mrs. Hormach was a nervous, demanding person who wanted perfection from everyone. We had a mixed class of girls and boys, and it took a long time for the teacher and students to get to know each other. Mrs. Hormach had a lot of problems with the boys and was always ready with her stick to punish them for the slightest disobedience. It didn't make matters any better that she dressed very formally; year after year, she wore the same colour and style of dress with her hair in a rigid braid. None of her students ever had a close relationship with her. She was simply the teacher, and we were afraid of her.

There were also fun activities at school. Because our town had a mineral hot spring with a beautiful bathhouse built over it, all the classes went swimming there regularly, boys and girls separately, under a teacher's supervision. Occasionally, the whole class also attended carefully selected movies, mainly French and American classics with Hungarian subtitles, but we needed to get permission from the principal to go. My favourite places were the town's two well-stocked libraries. Every Friday, I would select some books to bring home and could hardly wait to start reading them. My favourite subject in school was geography. I loved to explore different countries and places and to make maps. I became the best map-maker in my class, and this made me feel good because the teacher's approval was very important to me.

When I started my own dressmaking salon many years later, Mrs. Hormach became my best customer. We were still on formal terms, but she had mellowed over the years, and I was not afraid of her anymore, so we were able to have friendly discussions when she came in for fittings. She had a child with Down's syndrome and devoted all her energy to taking care of her. Mrs. Hormach died at a relatively early age and her child followed soon after. I missed her and mourned her passing, remembering all the knowledge she passed on to me.

## DAILY LIFE

As a teacher of Jewish religion and history, my father received a monthly salary from the state, but since teachers were never paid generously he had to manage his salary carefully to provide for his family, which grew to include two more brothers, Shimon and Menachem. Besides feeding and clothing his four children, there was always an extra mouth to feed at our house, since young yeshiva students from nearby villages often ate as guests at our table.

Most of the boys who went to the local yeshiva were from out of town. Tuition was free, and many of the boys who studied there came from poor families who couldn't pay for their keep, so the students lived in rented rooms and ate with members of the Jewish community, at a different house every day. In addition to the six of us, we had our regulars, two or three boys usually, and one on the Sabbath, who came to have their meals with us. These boys became part of our family and were like big brothers to us kids.

While my father provided our family's financial stability, my mother was in charge of our well-being. She was an excellent cook and a thrifty homemaker who managed Father's salary carefully to cover all the expenses needed for a growing family. Running a household with four children was a big task, and so we always had help in the house, usually a young girl from the nearby village who lived with us until she got married.

Everything was made at home in those days. Early every morning my mother prepared the dough for bread, which was then carried to the bakery to be baked in a large oven used by the whole community. Several grocery stores in town carried staple dry foods, but to get fresh fruit, vegetables, eggs, live chickens, ducks and geese, we had to rely on the women from the nearby villages and farms who brought their products to the market in town. These farm women walked long distances with their products on their backs to bring them to the marketplace in the centre of town and sat in the open on low stools, loudly praising their wares for the prospective customers. In bad weather, tents were erected. Part of the fun of buying at the market was the haggling, where everyone argued until both sides were satisfied with the deal. The place was noisy and smelly from the different types of merchandise but full of life.

We had no icebox, so the coolest place in the house was the cellar, which was where we stored the potatoes, onions and other vegetables. The live chickens we bought in the market were then taken to the slaughterhouse where they were plucked and prepared for the midday meals.

Summer was the busiest time in the kitchen. We helped Mother make jams, preserves and juices from the freshest fruit of the season, which she would store on the pantry shelves for the long winter ahead. When Mother brought home the first cherries of the season, I would place pairs of attached cherries over my ears, pretending they were pretty red earrings.

She also grated and salted cabbages and put them into large barrels to make sauerkraut. Grapes were hung from the ceiling in the pantry by bunches, and hundreds of kilograms of flour were put away for the winter. After all the peeling and cooking and the sterilizing of hundreds of bottles, the pantry looked like a well-stocked grocery store, and we kids looked forward to getting some treats from there every now and then for good behaviour.

Washday was another day of hard work. We had a woman who helped with the washing, Auntie Julia, who came regularly to wash and iron the linens, tablecloths and shirts. The elaborate process started early in the morning and turned the whole house upside down. Auntie Julia washed, boiled, bleached and starched everything in the kitchen before hanging it all in the attic to dry. In winter, the clothes froze on the line and took many days to dry but they had a beautiful fresh smell when we brought them down to be ironed. Ironing took another day or two. The fumes from the charcoal used to heat the iron often gave us headaches.

Even with so much to do at home, Mother still had time for charity work. She was part of a ladies' auxiliary in the Jewish community that took care of the needy and elderly who had no immediate families. She often visited sick neighbours and lonely older people who had no one to talk to. I would also regularly take meals to sick people with our maid.

The Jewish community took care of its people, including those in financial need. There was a hospitality house for the homeless and travellers who couldn't afford to pay for a hotel room. This house was looked after by a family in exchange for free rent. The Ladies' Auxiliary also took care of orphans and the bedridden elderly, with a different household responsible each day to feed and care for them. There was also a well-organized *chevra kadisha*, a volunteer burial society. Life was not always easy for everyone, with most Jews living in harsh conditions, but the community always sought to help those in need.

I remember an elderly couple, Mr. and Mrs. Laufer, who lived on our street in Szerencs and had no children of their own or other close relatives. He was a dance instructor, a very unusual profession for a Jewish man, and was a God-fearing man, short and agile with a good sense of humour. Mr. Laufer used to travel to remote farms and villages by foot, unless he was lucky enough to get a lift, bringing a breath of fresh air to the peasants by teaching them to dance and sharing all the new songs. The other children and I used to follow him around because he told us jokes and stories and always had some sweets in his pockets for us. He didn't take anything seriously and life for him was full of fun and enjoyment. He left all financial worries to his wife, a sweet, orderly and spotlessly clean woman. One day while her husband was away Mrs. Laufer got very ill. The neighbours came to help by bringing her food and doing the daily chores, but her condition worsened. When her husband finally came home, she was dying.

Mr. Laufer was devastated by his wife's death and wandered around like a lost child. Their house became quiet with no more singing and joking around. He sat by the window, deep in thought, and hardly spoke to anyone. The neighbours took turns providing meals for him, and when my mother's turn came to send in the daily provision, my younger brother Shimon and I took the food. We knocked on the door and stood by his doorway for a long time. When he finally opened it, we timidly waited for him to return our greetings. It seemed like he didn't even notice us so we just stood there not knowing what to do.

All of a sudden, Mr. Laufer came alive, called us in, ignored the food and started to tell us stories. We sat there as if hypnotized, listening to his every word. But, after a while, the spark was gone again and the house filled with the memories of Mrs. Laufer. A short while after this incident, he couldn't bear the loneliness any longer and died seemingly of a broken heart.

SPECIAL DAYS OF THE YEAR

The only day Mother really rested was the Sabbath. Since food was always prepared on Friday for the Sabbath, she was free to join the family at the synagogue on Saturday mornings. The synagogue, which stood in the middle of town, was an impressive building with a high domed ceiling. The ceiling was hand-painted a pretty blue colour and hanging from it were huge chandeliers that gave a special glow to the whole interior. My mother and I sat with all the women in the wraparound gallery along the second floor. Seats were numbered and reserved there, and since kids were not allowed to sit on them I would stand behind Mother's seat during services. In the afternoons, after services and the midday meal were done, her friends would come to visit. She served her guests fresh fruit, cakes and pretty bonbons while they sat talking, mostly about family matters.

When I was growing up, Purim was another busy time in our lives. We planned the *mishloach manot*, gift baskets of food, and the *seuda*, the festive meal, weeks ahead of time. Since I was the only girl in the family, I shared some of the responsibility with my mother to complete these chores, which were time-consuming and hard work.

Baking a cake was not as simple then as it is today. Everything was done by hand. My mother made a shopping list to take to the grocer and went early to the market to buy the eggs for the cakes and cookies. All the ingredients had to be gathered in the right order and the nuts had to be chopped, the chocolate grated. My brothers and I got to beat the egg whites to stiffness, a job we liked because we got to lick the bowls. By the day before Purim, the plates were filled with an assortment of cakes and cookies, all wrapped beautifully with my mother's handmade covers and ready to be distributed to friends and family in gift baskets.

In the early morning on the day of the holiday, we would listen to the *Megillah*, the Scroll of Esther, and, at lunchtime we children started to deliver the *mishloach manot*. We usually received a prize of sweets for our labour at the homes we visited, but if we were given money we had to give it away for *tzedakah*, charity. By the time we got back home, our house had become a very busy place. Mother was cooking the meal and Father was at home to welcome all the visitors, poor people and *yeshiva bochurs*, students of Jewish studies, who would be arriving for Purim. The *yeshiva bochurs* dressed in funny costumes and brought with them musicians who entertained us with rhymes, songs and skits. (The money they collected went to the poor.)

Everything was ready by early evening for the real treat, sharing our delicious meal with many poor people who were invited to be part of the celebrations. After supper, the whole congregation of our synagogue went out walking, calling on individual homes, singing, dancing and helping themselves to drinks and the abundance of cakes we had accumulated during the day. The merriment went on late into the night, and the next morning, which was *Shushan* Purim, brought with it even more dancing and singing.

We were exhausted by all this excitement and satiated by the rich cakes, which we had to finish to the last crumbs since Pesach cleaning was just around the corner.

NEW RESPONSIBILITIES

Mother used to visit her parents in Mezőkövesd, a train ride of several hours away, and we would have to carry on without her. When I was about twelve years old, she decided that, as the oldest child and the only daughter, I was old enough to take over the kitchen for a few days in her absence. She advised me on certain family rules so that Father and my brothers wouldn't starve or get sick from my scant knowledge of how to put a decent meal together.

I was very excited and felt grown-up when I became the chef with full kitchen authority in her absence. I asked my brothers what meal I should cook for my first time in charge of the kitchen. They all voted for bean soup, their favourite. I agreed. When I started to assemble the ingredients for the soup and tried to remember how Mother made it, I became apprehensive. Why hadn't I gotten the recipe from her before she left? Well, I was on my own and so I simply put everything I thought I needed for the soup into the pot. I put the fire on, started cooking and hoped for the best. One thing I did remember from Mother's talks with our neighbour on the subject of cooking beans was that it took a long time. Nervously, I set the table, made the salad, assembled the side dishes and waited for the family's return.

The boys and Father were hungry when they came home and watched me carefully as I ladled the soup into their bowls. Just one look at their faces as they tasted it and I guessed something was not right with my bean soup. I had forgotten to put salt into the cooking water. No matter what I tried to correct this mistake, the beans had no taste.

The teasing went on until I burst out crying and Father ordered my brothers to stop making fun of me. Being such a good man, he finished his plate of soup and told me it was the best soup he had ever eaten. I knew very well that he was just saying that to make me feel better, but I was so grateful for the kind words of my wonderful father. I was relieved when Mother returned home several days later loaded with gifts for everyone.

I loved to spend time in Father's office, which was adjacent to the synagogue. Helping him seal envelopes and stamp documents made me feel important. During the week, Father usually came home for the midday meal, had a short nap and then went back to work. When he came home again around eight in the evening, we had a light supper together. Mealtimes were very important. It was the time when the whole family sat together discussing the events of their day. We knew from an early age that we could never miss these family meals. After supper, Father supervised our homework and answered any questions we had about our school work and the world in general.

There was always lots to do in our town when we were kids. In the winter, we often had a visiting theatre group come to town, and in the summer the circus came. I particularly loved the tightrope walkers, but I worried about their safety up in the air as I watched them. There were also free evening concerts in the park in the summer. Most of the population came out to listen to these concerts, sitting on benches and socializing with friends while they listened to the music. The youths of the town walked up and down the main street, meeting with friends and having a good time.

March 15 was a national holiday in Hungary commemorating the 1848 Hungarian Revolution, and the town hung flags from most of the buildings on the main street to celebrate. We had special presentations in school where the entire student body marched to the music of a live band, followed by speeches and poetry readings. Children wore their spring outfits with pride, and we all had to wear ribbons with the national colours of the country. Because the weather was still on the cool side in March, the biggest issue for us girls was that we wanted to wear knee socks instead of full stockings, even though most girls' mothers insisted on the stockings. My mother was no different. Mother and I never failed to argue over whether I would wear the knee socks or not. The discussion went something like this:

Mother: "Judith, I absolutely forbid you to wear socks today."

Judith: "But Mamuka, it is warm outside. All my friends will be in knee socks and they will make fun of me for being different."

Mother: "I don't care what your friends are doing. You just recovered from your cold and missed many days of school. Do you want to be sick again?"

Judith: "Mamuka, please, I promise I won't be sick. The sun is shining, it is spring already, please let me be like my friends."

Mother: "No use arguing. Let's not make an issue out of the socks."

Judith: "All right! I will wear the stockings if you want me to be the laughing stock of the whole school."

A few hours later, I was back from school with a red nose and soaking wet from the sudden downpour while we were marching in the parade.

Mother: "What happened to you? Let me give you a hot drink. You look frozen. Let's take off your wet clothes. You see, you cannot trust this weather. It is still unpredictable this time of year."

Judith: "I am sorry, Mamuka, for the argument we had this morning. It seems mothers always know best."

YITZHAK

Father's meagre salary made life challenging in many ways. Teachers were never paid properly for their knowledge and talent in educating children, but Father was determined to pay for our schooling. Feeling it was his responsibility, Father found a way to send my brothers Yitzhak and Shimon out of town to study in a yeshiva. They had to find their own accommodations and food in the Jewish community, but we sent them extra packages of food whenever we could.

Yitzhak was an even-tempered and good-natured child, who was always full of laughter. His character fit his name, which means "laughing" in Hebrew. In the Bible, when Sarah, Abraham's wife, was told by the visiting angel that she would have a baby, she started to laugh. She couldn't believe that it was possible to conceive and birth a child at her age, since she was more than a hundred years old. When the baby was born, she called him Yitzhak.

He never caused our parents any aggravation, but a very painful episode did occur when Yitzhak was about eighteen years old. He was studying at a yeshiva in a nearby town and had come home for a Jewish holiday. He went to the *beit hamidrash*, the study house next to the synagogue, to study with his friends. As they were leaving, they encountered the mayor's son, who began teasing them with nasty antisemitic remarks. A proud young man, Yitzhak wasn't prepared to let him get away with these insults. There was a brawl, and my brother beat him up but lost a tooth in the process. When he came home bloodied and overwrought, he asked my father, "Why is he yelling that I am a dirty Jew? I didn't do anything to him. I just had to return his blows."

This was the only time I ever saw Yitzhak cry, and I felt the pain in my father's heart as he replied. "My son," he said, "I know that you are right. But remember, he is the mayor's son and we are Jews." As soon as the holiday was over, Father put him on a train back to the yeshiva because he was afraid of retaliation against all of the Jews in town.

As Yitzhak got older, he became too restless to sit and learn in the yeshiva. He used his guilt over our father's struggle to cover his expenses as leverage to win over our disapproving father. After a strong argument, Father reluctantly gave his blessing. Yitzhak found a job in the Jewish hospital in Budapest and enjoyed the freedom of being on his own. But Mother, a real worrier, felt that Yitzhak was still too young to live alone in a big city and travelled to the capital to check things out. While she was there, Yitzhak introduced her to a young woman named Flora, who was working in the hospital as a student nurse. Mother was very impressed by her fine character and later told us all about her and that she hoped her future daughter-in-law would be like her when the time came for Yitzhak to marry. This kindled a warm relationship between them.

## A SPECIAL INSURANCE AND A LIFELONG SKILL

Even with his small income and a large family to take care of, Father managed to put a few Hungarian *pengős* away each month into an insurance policy in my name so that there would be money for a simple trousseau and to make me a wedding.

My best friend, Sári, was enrolled in the teachers' seminary after high school, in a nearby city. She studied there only two years and came home claiming that school was boring, even though I was dying to continue my studies. Despite our different temperaments, Sári and I remained best friends.

Out of boredom, Sári decided to get married at nineteen. Unfortunately, her husband was not a good match for her. Ten years her senior, the workaholic dentist had a very dour and rigid temperament, so he was not an ideal partner for fun-loving Sári. After a few months of marriage, her husband was called into the army and was soon reported to be missing in action.

By that time, Sári was expecting her first child. Lonely and unhappy with a difficult pregnancy, she was miserable. She lost her baby.

The lively, fun-loving Sári became a recluse, hating the world and blaming it for her misfortune.

Although my heart had been set on higher learning like my brothers and Sári, being the eldest child and the only girl, and since my father couldn't afford to send me away to school, I was instead trained as a dressmaker. With my parents' blessing, I trained with a fine woman who had opened a salon a few years earlier. My father paid for a year of apprenticeship for me, and the following year I worked for free to develop the skills necessary to be a good seamstress.

I turned eighteen in 1938, the year I finished my training as a dressmaker. My original dream had been to be a teacher, but at this time conditions were deteriorating for Jews, which made it almost impossible for Jews to aim for higher education, even if my father could afford to pay for it. War was looming on the horizon and inflation was rampant — the only chance I had to earn some money and help my parents was to use my new skills as a dressmaker.

Being so young, I was very confident of my ability to run a workshop on my own and slowly headed in the right direction through trial and error. My parents bought me a sewing machine and let me have a room in our house as a workshop. Four young girls joined me as trainees and we created a pleasant atmosphere, joking and singing as we worked. I occasionally went to Budapest to visit my former teacher, who had opened a salon there, so I could learn some new ideas from her.

Trying to satisfy the different kinds of customers who knew little or nothing about how a garment should look on them caused me great headaches. Usually I just had to smile and agree because the customers were always right. Little by little, though, I gained more self-confidence and experience as I learned from my own mistakes.

When I cut and sewed a velvet garment, for example, the dress looked fine, except that when it was finished every part was a different shade. The customer who had ordered that particular dress was an old friend of my mother's and taught me the elementary rule of how to cut velvet — the pile of the material always has to run in the same direction. She was very nice about my mistakes, and I learned a lesson for a lifetime.

Life was peaceful and calm in Szerencs, and I treasure these bittersweet memories.

# The Delights of Family

MY MATERNAL GRANDPARENTS

My maternal grandfather, Aryeh Leib Hofstadter, came from a large family in the town of Dukla, in Galicia, which was part of the Austro-Hungarian Empire. Unfortunately, all the armies of Europe marched through that little town to reach the front lines in wartime, so Dukla was occupied many times by many different regimes. Every time a conqueror took the town, the population suffered, especially the Jews. That was the main reason my grandfather and his family left, seeking their livelihood elsewhere. Some of his brothers and sisters settled in Hungary; others moved to areas of Hungary that are now Yugoslavia and Czechoslovakia, as well as to America. But they were a close-knit, loving family and kept in touch and visited each other as often as border restrictions and their financial circumstances allowed.

Grandpa Aryeh Leib was very young when he married our grandma, Feige Leah Biron, who came from the same town as Grandpa. Right after their marriage, they settled in Mezőkövesd in Hungary and raised eleven children — four sons and seven daughters: Wili Zev, Heszu Yechezkel, Moshe, Jeno Yaakov, Malvin (Schiffman), Rivka (Weisz), Sári (Luger), Bella (Bokor), Puncsi Sorel (Adler), Rózsi Rachel (Schwarcz) and Chana (Ungar). Their youngest daughter, Chana, was born when they already had a few grandchildren. Grandpa was a good father and provider for his family. At the beginning of his marriage, he made a living as a shochet, a ritual slaughterer, but having a good business sense, he soon became a storekeeper and made a comfortable living.

Grandpa was a very religious, God-fearing and good-hearted man. He loved to sing and dance, usually solo, and loved to be the centre of attention. When he attended a family or friend's wedding, he instantly became the life of the party. He was bright, friendly and outgoing. A very polite man, Grandpa greeted both young and old with a smile and friendly words. He respected knowledge and good manners but had no patience for stupidity. He had a quick temper that flared up easily but never for long. With his quick mind, he judged people accurately. If he did not like someone, he didn't bother with them.

Borders were no barriers for him, and he travelled constantly, visiting his brothers and sisters in different countries. With his ability to speak Yiddish, he managed to go as far as America, where he stayed for a year and then came back, saying that the atmosphere in the United States was not to his liking. But he brought modern machinery back with him and established a matzah bakery, which he managed very successfully. Well liked by both Jews and non-Jews, he received a medal and citation from the Hungarian government as an outstanding citizen. Once, when Grandpa was visiting a cousin in Italy, the mayor of Mezőkövesd sent him a telegram calling him home. An election had been called and my grandfather's influence over the Jewish community was important for the mayor to win the election.

Grandpa tried to instill the love of learning in his sons and went out of his way to provide the necessities to allow them to stay in the yeshiva and study. He had strict authority over his children's lives even when his sons grew up, married and moved to different cities. His daughters all married God-fearing, educated men, who were handpicked by Grandpa. His sons-in-law loved and respected him for his sincerity, quick wit and generosity with his time and money.

He visited his children regularly to see if everything was in good order. As soon as he felt satisfied that all was well, he was ready to move on to the next destination, usually another family visit. He even treated his grandchildren this way. He used to line us up and ask us questions about our schoolwork and, as we grew older, about our work. He wanted to know everything that went on in his family.

He was naturally inclined to do favours for anyone in need. If anyone he knew was in financial trouble, Grandpa was there to bail them out, never remembering to whom he had lent the money.

A strong friendship existed between my grandfather and Mordechai Rubinstein, a fellow businessman, from the village of Szentistván, eight kilometres from Mezőkövesd. Together the two friends created their own "Mitzvah Club" to help the poor in a private way. Each morning, Mr. Rubinstein walked to the synagogue for prayers and met my grandpa. Since they were semi-retired, they had time to study the Talmud and involve themselves in community activities.

From week to week, their routine rarely varied. Every Monday morning, the pair paid a visit to a few well-to-do Jews to collect money on behalf of the struggling families who sold merchandise in the markets in nearby villages. On Tuesdays, these families received the money as a loan and went to the wholesalers to buy goods to sell in the bazaar. On Wednesday evenings, they travelled to their destinations in covered, horse-drawn carriages, and on Thursday mornings they set up their tables and began waiting for customers. On their way home that evening, these sellers stopped to repay the borrowed money to the two partners who then returned the money to the original donors. In this way, poor people were able to sell merchandise and earn enough profit to buy food for their families and everybody was happy. The following Monday, the cycle started again. Many of the less fortunate lived this way, relying on the weekly loan to help them make a decent living for their families. Mr. Rubinstein passed away in his early eighties, but his son Béla would later become my dear husband and life partner.

When the political situation deteriorated in Hungary, my grand-father became very depressed and feared the worst. He bought all the antisemitic newspapers, studied them carefully and predicted that all would not end well. Unfortunately, his pessimism was well-founded. My grandfather was a great and righteous man, and three of his great-grandchildren have been named after him.

My maternal grandmother, Feige Leah Biron, had a great influ-ence on me growing up. She was a petite, pretty woman with a clear complexion who never touched makeup, not even a simple cream. Always dressed modestly in black or navy, with laced high shoes, she commanded respect by showing respect for others. Like her husband, she was deeply religious, with her prayer book always at hand.

After finishing her multitude of daily chores, she would read to us from her precious *Tsena u'Rena*, popularly known as the women's Bible. Because it was written in Yiddish, we didn't understand a word of what she was reading, but we nonetheless had to sit and listen to her singsong intonation of the stories of our people. Because she and Grandpa had moved to Hungary from their native Galicia right after they married, she had no relatives or friends in the strange land when she came and had a difficult time adjusting, especially to the language. She never learned the proper use of the Hungarian language, which bothered her. Interestingly, though, we communicated with her quite well, since children adapt to situations much more easily.

Raising eleven children, she had no time for idleness. She was a doer and a nurturer. I never saw her sitting still, except on the Sab-bath, when she allowed herself the luxury of taking it easy. Every Fri-day night after prayer services, their married children came to my grandparents' house with their own families to pay their respects and wish them a good Sabbath. Grandma was ready for them and served her freshly baked delicacies, and everybody had a good time.

Grandma was a very pretty older woman who was as gracious as Queen Victoria. She had a six-strand necklace of sweet-water pearls, a gift from Grandpa at their engagement, that she used to wear on special occasions. All of her granddaughters admired the necklace, which looked so lovely when she was wearing it. She promised us that, after her death, we would share it. Often the threads would loosen, and she lost a few of the pearls, so over time the strands got smaller. But her pearls still looked good on her.

The moment school was out, we started packing, ready to head to our grandparents' home in Mezőkövesd to spend some of the summer holidays with them. Other grandchildren also came to my grandparents' house from different cities, filling it with laughter as we joked around for Grandma's delight. Some of us travelled a long distance to get there, but it always was a happy reunion to meet the clan. We hardly had time to settle down before Grandma, our general manager, gave out the assignments for our daily tasks, which included helping out in the kitchen, peeling vegetables and dusting the furniture. Even with the help, though, Grandma was in constant motion, cooking, baking and serving her delicious meals to the always-hungry grandchildren.

During the long, hot summer afternoons, we would rather stay indoors in the cool rooms and play quietly so as not to disturb our grandparents' "siesta."

My grandparents' big house had rooms with high ceilings, large windows with wooden shutters and double doors, but my favourite room was the so-called salon, which was used only on special occasions. It was a beautiful room where the ceiling was painted with a colourful floral design. It had a black iron stove in the corner and was filled with large pieces of upholstered furniture. I loved to cuddle up in one of the big armchairs that had needlepoint upholstery and mother-of-pearl buttons all around the edges. Many times I fell asleep in that cozy chair after we had finished telling stories to each other in the semi-darkness.

Thursdays were the only days we disliked at Grandma's house. That was the day she turned her kitchen upside down with her vigorous cleaning. Her baking sheets, jelly-mould sets and heavy stainless steel cooking pots and pans had to be polished to a shine. Her kitchen smelled fresh and clean afterwards, and as a reward for our hard work we got a special treat, usually her freshly baked cookies and permission to go out to play with our friends who were waiting patiently for us by the gate.

Grandma loved music, and at twilight we sat on the steps of her veranda singing the latest hit parade songs for her. In return, she sang to us her favourite Yiddish songs, which we didn't understand, but we listened intently anyway because they were her songs and meant so much to her. We were too young to understand the yearning she expressed in her songs, being so far from her own family in Galicia. As summer ended, one by one we returned to our homes promising each other to return the next summer.

In the winter months, their big house was empty. Grandpa had a restless nature and could not stand the quiet. He loved to travel and would visit his children often in their different cities to check on his family's well-being. Grandma was a compulsive cleaner, which irritated Grandpa a lot, so she took the opportunity when he was away to do her general cleaning.

## PATERNAL GRANDPARENTS

My paternal grandfather, Eliezer Menachem Mendel Schwarcz, was born in the town of Zalozce in Galicia. According to family history, our ancestors originally came from Spain and were expelled during the Inquisition because they were unwilling to convert to Catholicism. It was easy at that time to cross borders from one country to another, and my ancestors wandered through half of Europe before settling in Galicia. Grandpa's family eventually ended up in Mezőlaborc, a small town in Czechoslovakia.

Grandpa was a brilliant scholar who studied in the best yeshivas. He was a handsome man with deep blue eyes, an even temper and a tall, erect posture. He was also a fine human being. He had two sisters and one brother who lived in different cities but they corresponded constantly to keep in touch.

When Grandpa reached a marriageable age, his future father-in-law, Yitzhak Bezalel Sekler, visited the yeshiva where he was studying seeking the best *Yeshiva bochur* as a husband for his daughter. The head of the yeshiva suggested Eliezer, who was his prize student. Yitzhak met my grandfather, was satisfied, and then the young people met and decided to get married.

His daughter, my grandma Julia Yehudis Sekler, was born in Dukla, Galicia, where her father was the town's *feldsher*, a medical doctor without a diploma. He was a pious man with a great knowledge of the sciences and general studies. He was so respected that the doctors in town used to invite him for consultations on difficult cases because they trusted his wisdom and experience

The young couple settled in Hungary in the town of Tiszadob where Grandpa, like my maternal grandfather, earned a living as a shochet. They had seven children — six boys and one girl: Elias Eliyahu, Yechezkel, Yaakov (Janki), Herman, Shlomie (Solomon), one boy whose name I can't recall and Ethel. There were three more children who died from childhood diseases. As the children grew, Grandpa and Grandma opened a grocery store and the older boys helped run the business. But Grandpa's greatest love was his books. He taught himself French and English and educated his sons at home with great patience and love. He was a perfect role model for them to follow.

When their youngest child, Shlomie, was just a baby, tragedy struck and Grandma Yehudit became seriously ill. She travelled home to seek help from her father who took her to Vienna to see the leading doctors. But, unfortunately, her breast cancer was so advanced by that time that she was beyond help. She died shortly after and was buried in her hometown.

Grandpa was devastated by his great loss. He was not capable of taking care of his large family and also running the business on his own, so when his daughter, my aunt Ethel, married at a very early age, she took two of her little brothers with her and raised them as her own. Even so, Grandpa had too many remaining children to be able to give them a stable home life. He married a young widow who had a baby boy and whose husband had been killed while he was helping a neighbour whose house was on fire. Together they raised the rest of the boys until, one by one, they left the family nest.

By that time, they had moved to a bigger town, Mezőcsát, where the boys had a better opportunity to make a living while Grandpa still ran a grocery store. Unfortunately, his second wife died in the typhus epidemic that spread through the town when she was in her late seventies. Grandpa moved to his youngest son's house, where Uncle Solomon, Aunt Paula and their lively kids took loving care of him.

My paternal grandfather died at the age of eighty-four, worn out from living; he left a wonderful legacy for his children and numerous grandchildren. His love for learning and his respect for everybody made him a very special person.

He was buried in Mezőcsát. May his *neshama*, his soul, rest in peace for he was a man respected by everyone.

## AUNT ETHEL'S WEDDING

My aunt Ethel, Father's only sister, married very young, and her wedding day had a dramatic story that my parents often told us children about.

My grandfather and his family were living near the Tisza River, a fast-flowing river with few bridges connecting their town, Mezőcsát, to the villages on the other side. Aunt Ethel's wedding day was in the early spring when the river, filled with spring rain, flooded the surrounding areas and washed away the bridges.

The bride, Ethel, was dressed in her finery and waited for her groom. But as the clock ticked away, there was no sign of the groom, and the wedding guests began getting nervous. The tension grew and Ethel started to cry when evening came and there was still no sign of the groom's wedding party. Finally, the village guests went home to eat their supper and rumours flew as to the different possibilities of why the groom was absent.

Around midnight, a faint sound of music was heard in the distance. To everybody's relief, as the music grew louder, the groom arrived followed by a Roma band and torch carriers. He had been delayed due to the washed-out bridges. The chuppah, the wedding canopy, was set up and the ceremony began. The eating, singing and dancing went on all night. Late the next morning, after prayers and a good breakfast, the out-of-town guests said their thanks and left, followed by the tired Roma who were still playing. The dust had hardly settled when the wedding guests from the other side of the village returned. Lunch was served and singing and dancing followed. The merriment went on until, finally, they left for home and the party was finally over.

## COUSINS

Living in Szerencs meant that I was separated from my family in Mezőcsát, from my grandparents, uncles, aunts and many cousins, so visiting them was very important to me. I was close to Uncle Herman's children, especially my dear cousins Nick and Nellie, and the highlight of the year became the four weeks I spent with Nellie and Nick every summer in Mezőcsát. Nick was the youngest child in his family and had an angel's face and a mischievous personality. Nellie and I argued frequently, as little girls do, but Nick was our hero, our knight in shining armour. We were impressed by his bravado — nobody could outdo Nick when it came to climbing trees or sliding down from the rooftops of their family home. We watched him with awe as he dangled his feet from the rafters, smiling to show us how brave he was. It was a wonder that he never had any serious injuries, although he often needed to be taken to see the woman we called Aunt Elizabeth, a peasant who treated his many cuts and bruises with special potions straight out of her kitchen.

Uncle Herman was in the United States, and his wife, Aunt Czili, was busy taking care of her growing flock of children. Auntie was smart and efficient, but she had very little time to monitor our summer activities. So, we did as we pleased and had a great time doing it. My gentle paternal grandfather showered us with love and attention and trusted us completely. It never occurred to him to notice our outlandish behaviour.

Nick and Nellie also had a brother, Ernő, and two sisters, Irene and Ilus. My cousin Ilus was a pretty child and very much aware of it. Her ambition to better herself intellectually was limited, but her beauty made her feel she had every right to be spoiled and catered to.

When she was about fourteen, she developed back trouble and had to lie in a cast on her back for a whole year. In the beginning, she was inconsolable. During the summer, her older brothers carried her out to the back porch where she held court for friends, but in the winter she was locked in her little room, feeling bitter about her situation. Her friends' visits became less frequent, and she was left alone a great deal. Her family was busy with their own lives and her little mirror became her only solace and companion. She used to look at and talk to herself, planning and dreaming of the day when she would get out of her miserable condition.

Since her father was in America at that time working hard and saving every penny he made, sending money home to secure a better life for his family, and her mother was busy with their little grocery store and taking care of the family, neither of her parents were able to entertain their bored daughter. My own father had become the children's guardian in their father's absence and used to carry Ilus in his arms to the hospital for her checkups. Everybody tried to be kind and compassionate to her but, still, she was alone a lot and she found it hard to dream of a better future.

Finally the cast came off, her back got better and she started to blossom. Trying to make up for lost time, she enjoyed her new life to the fullest, ignored her responsibilities and didn't help out around the house. She loved pretty clothes and concentrated on being admired by the many young men who surrounded her constantly. She felt that the whole world owed her compensation for the time she had been imprisoned in the cast.

Eventually, she married Dezső Reich, a very serious, intelligent man, the only son of a father who spoiled him. He loved Ilus in his own way and was a good provider who catered to her every whim. Since they had no children, all her energy was channelled into taking care of herself first, then her husband and their pretty apartment. She dressed very well and loved going in to town to shop. She attended concerts and the theatre and generally enjoyed having a good time. At the beginning of their marriage, her husband felt it was his duty to escort her when she went out, but his love for books and learning was so great that a pattern slowly developed in their marriage. She would go out in the evenings with her friends to movies, theatres, concerts or just for a cup of coffee in the coffee houses where music was playing and would have a great time dancing, while her husband stayed home to read and study. Her house looked like a dollhouse, because she had excellent taste and was a good homemaker. She never worked and spent all her time taking care of herself.

As I was growing up, my parents allowed me to visit Ilus and Dezső occasionally. It was my greatest pleasure to stay with them. I almost worshipped my cousin's sophisticated ways. Whatever she did or said was great in my eyes. I was about sixteen at the time, an only daughter, and wanted to have a sister of my own. She took me shopping and introduced me to her colourful friends. We talked a lot about things that interested me and she was fun to be with.

My relationships with these cousins changed over time. Nick was eventually sent out of town to study in a yeshiva, after which Nellie and I had little time for foolishness anymore. When Uncle Herman returned home from America, the Hungarian government began to give him trouble because he had become an American citizen. The Hungarians didn't want Americans living in Hungary, and life was becoming more difficult for Hungarian Jews, and so he decided to leave Hungary with his wife and all of their children except for Ilus, who stayed behind in Hungary with her husband, Dezső.

I remember clearly how we felt when we received the telegram informing us of their sudden departure. My father took the first train to catch them at the border to say goodbye, but their train had already left one hour earlier. Unfortunately, they never met again.

# War Comes to Szerencs

We were still in our home when the first young Jewish men were sent into forced labour after Hungary established a forced-labour service in 1939. As hard as things had been before the war, the general situation got worse, especially for Jews, when World War II started in September 1939. A year later, in November 1940, Hungary officially became an ally to the Nazi regime. Hungary joined with Hitler because the country hoped that he would restore Hungary to its old glory, since he promised to return the territories that had been taken away from Hungary by the 1920 Treaty of Trianon, which was signed by the United States, England and France at the end of World War I. That treaty agreement had been a tragedy for Hungary.

Father, being a deeply religious and trusting person, hoped for an early end to the war and kept up the monthly payments to the insurance company despite rising inflation, and we continued to live as best we could. But, by 1944, the situation was becoming increasingly chaotic for Jews in Hungary, as children were expelled from schools and Jews were dismissed from their jobs and cut off from their government salaries.

Before Pesach in 1944, I went to visit my maternal grandparents. My grandmother always treated me like I was special, her daughter's only daughter, and she said I was gentler and more appreciative than the others. She had written to me and asked when I was coming, and my mother urged me to go. So I left everything at home and went to visit for a few days. I made her a dress, which she really appreciated. We sang and talked, and when it was time for me to go she asked me, "My child, when will I see you again?" It seemed that somehow, she felt something ominous was in the air.

It was very hard for me to leave her, but I didn't understand why I felt this way. As I looked out the window of the train, for the first time I saw German soldiers in Hungary and their presence gave me shivers. You could feel the discomfort on the train — no one seemed to know what was happening. When I got home late that night, my father was waiting for me at the station. I told him about my trip and went to sleep. The next morning, my father came home with a long face and the sad news that the Nazis had moved into Hungary. The date was Sunday, March 19, 1944. By the following morning, the Nazis were marching all over our town and there was a whole battalion on the main road.

Life began to change very quickly. Only weeks later, we received the order that every Jew had to wear a yellow star and that anyone caught without it would be imprisoned. At first we thought it was a joke but soon found that it was very serious. Everyone needed a yellow star, and the textile stores were soon sold out, and I was kept busy cutting out yellow material. Then the restrictions came: the Jews couldn't do this, the Jews couldn't do that.

My father, like the rabbi, the *chazzan*, or cantor, and the shochet, was a paid employee of the Jewish community and had an office in which he kept all the records of the community — who was born, who was married, who had died. Unfortunately, the Nazis demanded that he give them a list of all the Jews in the city, even those staying as guests during Pesach. He was too frightened of retaliation not to comply and was tortured with guilt afterwards. He cried the whole night.

Father was also involved with the rescue committee. Refugees came from Vienna and then later on from Poland, and Father would hide them for the night in the *aron-koydesh*, the Holy Ark, in the synagogue. The next morning, he would send them with money and tickets to Budapest, where it was easier to hide or from where it was possible to still leave the country. At the time, several boats were leaving Budapest, carrying European Jews to British Mandate Palestine.

Once, my father went to Budapest to assist some refugees, and when he got back my mother turned to him bitterly.

"Why do you do favours for everyone but us?" she asked. "When will it be our turn to leave?"

"A captain cannot leave a sinking ship," he replied. "We have to wait until everybody has been saved."

Preparations for that Pesach went on as planned. Every corner of our house was cleaned. Tablecloths were freshly washed, starched and ironed. Candlesticks were polished until they gleamed. The children brought down the special Pesach dishes from the attic and set the table the way we always had in years before. We were only allowed to do our shopping during a certain time of day due to new restrictions and we went with fear in our hearts and the degrading yellow stars on our sleeves. Our spirits were crushed, and we had no joy to welcome the forthcoming holiday.

My father conducted the seder, the ceremonial Pesach meal, with all the dignity and hope he could muster. He explained the Exodus and the burdens our ancestors had to bear under the hard-hearted rulers of Egypt. While we were reading and listening to the story of how Moses led the former slaves to freedom, we felt a faint hope that maybe we too would be taken out of bondage soon and our nightmare would end. Our tears flowed as we felt our own misery. After the seder, my brave and practical mother still put away our Pesach dishes and set the house in order, pretending that all this nonsense was just temporary.

After midnight, with my younger brothers tucked into bed, sleep eluded me and I could see Father still praying in the other room, begging God for a miracle. The flickering candlelight made him an eerie figure in his white *kittel*, a ceremonial cloak that was customary in our family. I was crying bitterly, feeling helpless and sorry for all of us.

One of my best customers at that time was a young gentile woman whose husband was a high-ranking officer in the Hungarian army.

She was known to be a rabid antisemite but she was very pleasant to me and paid promptly — we never discussed politics. On what turned out to be the eve of our deportation to the ghetto, I still had a few pieces of her material in my workshop and didn't know how to get them back to her since we were forbidden to leave our homes. Without a word of sympathy or explanation, she sent one of her husband's men to get back her material, and I was really hurt by her indifference.

Right after the holiday, our precious family was torn apart. On April 16, 1944, I was taken with my parents and my younger brothers from our home by police. All of the other Jews of Szerencs were also rounded up. Each of us was allowed to take a bundle on our back, no more. We were ordered to go to the city hall and from there they took us to the train station. As we marched down the middle of the road toward the railway station, our good Christian neighbours watched without protest. Some were looking down, embarrassed maybe, but no helping hands or words of sympathy came our way. As long as I live, I will never forget the faces of the townspeople who watched us go. No one protested; no one said a thing. Some of our Jewish families were quite wealthy and had beautiful homes. The police locked the doors and put up signs forbidding anybody to enter but, no doubt, those who watched us being marched out of town were thinking about what was being left behind by their Jewish neighbours.

Among the town's newly emerged fascist sympathizers was a half-orphan, a young boy whose mother we called Aunt Julia and who had done our family's big monthly wash. They were poor and my mother had taken pity on the boy, fed him regularly and given him clothes. When the anti-Jewish terror began, Aunt Julia's son became a big shot in the Nazi-collaborationist Arrow Cross Party. Wearing a uniform and carrying a gun, he was full of hatred toward Jews. Perhaps he was among those who watched the entire Jewish population of our town walk dejectedly down the main road toward the dark, unknown fate that awaited us.

# Miseries and Miracles

My father, mother, sixteen-year-old brother Shimon, six-year-old Menachem and I, at twenty-four years old, were taken to the railway station with thousands of other wretched human beings. We boarded the train with no idea where we were going. The police locked and sealed the doors on the train. We became prisoners and were treated like criminals.

We were taken to Miskolc, a city containing a ghetto that held eleven thousand Jews. It was overcrowded with people who had been brought in from the neighbouring towns and villages, so hunger and sickness were rampant. In the ghetto, we suffered from hunger and the loss of human dignity. My mother had a sister, Rifka, who lived in the town, and we were fortunate to be able to stay in a corner of my aunt's house. Among the many others who were also crammed into her house was a very nice young family who had lived near us in Szerencs. Yitzhak Schonfeld had run a printing shop, and his wife, Rachel, took care of their three small children. The oldest was a boy of five, the middle child, Susy, was three and the baby had just been born when the Nazis transported all of the town's Jewish population to the ghetto.

Rachel was very busy taking care of her little flock, but since her baby was colicky she had little time to look after the older ones. From the first day we arrived, I formed a special bond with little Susy. She was a lovely child with big, round eyes, dimples and a head of rust-coloured ringlets. I couldn't resist her charm. The poor neglected child was looking for someone to pay attention to her needs, and I was happy to oblige. She followed me around demanding a good story when she was tired and would often fall asleep on my lap.

We shared our one room with the entire Zimmerman family. I had been a young teenager when they moved to our town of Szerencs. Although our families had been neighbours in Szerencs, I didn't know the son, Béla, very well at the time. I knew only that he was a friendly and pleasant person, much liked and respected by his friends and family.

Our shared tragedy had brought us together. We tried to help one another in this terrible situation. We became neighbours once again, but this was very different than Szerencs. Béla was not with us when we first arrived at the ghetto. His unit of the labour battalion arrived a few weeks later and worked at the railway station. Entering the ghetto was strictly forbidden to him and his friends, but they found ways to smuggle themselves in for a few minutes, knowing full well the consequences if they were caught. Béla and his friends brought us whatever food they were able to buy on the black market in town and tried to alleviate the pain, misery and hunger experienced by all of us in the ghetto.

We were all incredibly fearful, not knowing what would happen to us in the future; we also lacked privacy and personal space, all of which made everyone uneasy. With patience and cheerful attitudes, these men tried to keep us calm, which became the most important aspect of their visits. Each of their visits felt like a breath of fresh air.

After the police sealed the ghetto we all became victims of their inhumane treatment. They immediately selected ten elderly Jewish men to form the Judenrat, the council of Jewish leaders responsible for carrying out their orders. It was still cold and rainy in early April, but most of the people in the ghetto had to sleep in open sheds belonging to brick factories.

Although our misery there was ever-present, Jews in the ghetto found ways to help each other. A makeshift hospital was set up for the sick and elderly, and because of the immense hunger a soup kitchen was established. Once, the police even let a few young men go back to our former home under police escort and opened our houses so they could bring back food supplies to give out to the hungry masses.

Then the selections began. The police let the Jewish patients out of the mental hospital and allowed them loose in the ghetto. When the selection started, these unfortunate people were the first to be thrown into the cattle cars. House-to-house searches for victims made it impossible for anyone to escape.

Our family's turn for deportation came in the early summer of 1944. The misery of life in the ghetto had lasted a month before the order came to be relocated. The day before our departure, Béla brought us a large container of fruit marmalade that we took with us. The little children especially suffered, crying for water, which was unavailable to us. The marmalade helped to moisten their parched lips and we blessed Béla for his foresight and kindness. We were taken to the train station, jammed into cattle cars that were filled to the brim with human cargo and promised that we were being sent to Germany to work in the factories for the war effort and the greater glory of National Socialism. Of course, what they told us was a lie. Little did we know that our fate had already been sealed — the murderers had more sinister plans for us. Our possessions were replaced by a small bundle of food. We were given one loaf of bread and one large container of water per family and another container to serve as a toilet.

One woman, whose husband had been the shochet in town years before, was mentally ill and didn't understand what was happening. The police came and threw her in with our transport, but she refused to go. The police ordered several strong, healthy Jewish men to grab her. Two took her legs and two held her hands and she screamed as they carried her in. It was a pathetic, horrible sight. They threw her into the wagon next to ours, and I heard her crying during the entire journey. No one could get her to stop crying. Many times in my sleep, years later, I have heard her cries from that train car.

The cattle train left the ghetto tightly packed with its miserable cargo of hungry and worried people who didn't know their destination. By the time we crossed the border, we realized we were not going to Germany to work for the war effort as they had promised. We were in Poland and nobody had any idea where we were going or why.

For two awful nights and one day, the hunger, thirst and lack of privacy made the journey a nightmare. After travelling under the most degrading conditions, broken in spirit, hungry, dying of thirst and stripped of our human dignity, we finally arrived in Auschwitz-Birkenau, a place we had never heard of before.

It was June 16, 1944, a bright sunny day, when the doors were opened and we saw that we were surrounded by Jewish prisoners wearing striped uniforms and Nazi soldiers with their guns ready. Before our family left the trains and the women were separated from the men and the elderly, my father blessed me and instructed me to eat whatever they gave us. He also advised me to be among the first to offer to go to work and to try and get into a working crew because that might save my life. His intuitions were sound, but I am sure my father knew more about our situation than he told us. He just didn't want to frighten us.

We were pulled down from the cattle cars and the selection began. On the platform, excellent music played by inmates in striped uniforms welcomed us. By the fence, Nazi soldiers were waiting for the sick and feeble, promising to take them to the hospital right away. Another lie. They were thrown into what looked like ambulances, and we found out later that they had been immediately taken to the gas chambers and gassed instantly. Next came the mothers with small children. The Jewish inmates warned the mothers with children to give their children to their elderly relatives to try to save themselves but hardly anyone listened and almost all of them were killed. A few minutes later, my father disappeared with my brother Shimon, and I never saw them again.

As I was standing huddled with my mother and little brother, along came a high-ranking SS officer, who we later found out was Dr. Josef Mengele, the Nazis' infamous Angel of Death, and he started the selection among the women. He sent all of the older women to one side, separating them from the young, healthy-looking younger women. All those in the latter category went to the other side where they lined up, five in a row.

Her maternal instinct must have inspired my mother to do what she did next. In front of us stood four tall, good-looking girls, whom we knew from the ghetto. They were holding hands with three children, their little nieces and nephew, whose parents were hiding in Budapest. My mother pulled the children to her side and pushed me to be the fifth in the row with the four girls. "I will take care of the children" she told them, "and you take care of Judith."

I started to protest and turned around to go back to her, but within a minute my mother had disappeared with the three small children and my little brother. That was the last time I saw her. I often wonder how she knew she would save my life by separating me from herself and the children. It gives me sleepless nights even today when I think of the agony she went through before she was killed with those children, along with so many other innocents.

Dr. Mengele and his cronies quickly selected the young and healthy men and women. The rest were murdered within a few hours. We were herded toward the bathhouse to then endure the indignity of standing naked, having our hair cut off and given a quick cold shower. That immediate transformation left us in shock. We did not even recognize our best friends. Finally, we were led to the barracks, our new sleeping quarters.

Everything was very primitive in Auschwitz-Birkenau. The barracks were made of wood with tiny windows and approximately a thousand women were crowded into each barracks. Instead of conventional beds, there were only bunk beds that looked just like shelves, two or three tiers deep, covered with straw. The section where I slept had two tiers because of the low ceiling. The women were crammed together, row upon row.

The toilets were behind the barracks and consisted of a long wooden box with holes cut in the middle. The use of these toilets was tightly controlled. The Germans put us in a line and let in a certain number of women at a time. We had to be fast and get out quickly. If a person had diarrhea, the SS soldier who came for inspection every morning would send that person to be gassed right away.

Three weeks after I arrived, I was among 150 Hungarian Jewish women selected for labour in a part of the camp called Kanada. This was a warehouse for sorting out the bundles and suitcases that the unfortunate people had brought with them on their final journey. In large sheds, mountains of clothes, shoes and household articles were piled up, and we had to sort everything and package it into bundles to be shipped to Germany. On occasion, there was a painful situation when one of the workers found pictures or personal items that had belonged to their closest relatives and they knew very well what had happened to those poor people. This happened to me once. As I opened a bundle of clothes, a pretty little red-and-white polka-dotted dress stared up at me. I stood there frozen, recognizing the dress that had belonged to my darling little Susy, who I had taken care of in the ghetto. The tears started to flow from my eyes and I said a silent prayer for that innocent, beautiful child who I knew had been gassed along with her parents.

On a starvation diet and fearing for our lives every minute, we were frightened and hungry all the time, and the long hours of hard work took their toll on our mental and physical well-being. Eventually, I was among a handful of young people chosen to work on a road-building crew, part of a group of girls directed to carry stones from a bombed-out house that we had to dismantle with our bare hands.

Our only sense of hope came from the fleeting contact we had with other prisoners in the camp who were from our towns back home. It was strictly forbidden for the men housed on the other side of the camp to talk to us, but occasionally we were able to exchange a few words with those who came into our part of the camp to work as electricians or plumbers. One day, a young man in a striped uniform came in with the crew and I had a feeling that I knew him from somewhere. Before I had a chance to utter a word, he called out in Hungarian, "Who are you and where did you come from?"

"I am from Szerencs," I answered, and he started to cry.

"Do you remember me? I am Yossi Mangel. I hoped and prayed that at least your people might be spared this terrible ordeal."

I wanted to know what happened to his family and his answer was chilling. "They are all dead now. I don't think we will be alive here too long either."

We both cried then for our lost youth, our lost families and the terrible tragedy that was happening to our people. I never saw Yossi again but I hope and pray that, by some miracle, he made it.

While on our way to work one sunny morning in July 1944, we met a group of men in striped prison garb. As they passed, we heard their slow murmur in Hungarian and got very excited, thinking we might know someone among them. By the time we realized they were speaking Hungarian, we had already passed them, but we knew we would meet them again in following days. Although the guards marching with us strictly forbade any contact, we established a system to pass messages to them and to receive responses the next day.

A man I had never met before was marching in the middle of their column and he passed his questions along by a few friends who marched behind him. I was way out of hearing range to speak to him directly but I got his message through his friends. That's how I discovered he was a friend of my father's. The following morning, I answered him the same way.

One morning, a large onion flew through the air, directed at me. My father's friend had thrown it to me. My friends caught it, and I became the happy owner of a whole onion. That night, after work, we had a celebration. The onion was sliced into small pieces and I shared it with all my friends. It lifted our spirits a little and gave us some hope for a better tomorrow. I only saw that man one more time before he disappeared, never to be liberated from our miserable existence, except perhaps by death.

In July or August 1944, I was working with a road-building crew of 150 young women when a group of about a thousand Soviet army prisoners of war arrived in Auschwitz-Birkenau. We, the women on the other side of the high-voltage electric fence, got used to seeing them every morning as we marched to our working places. They were tall, blond, good-looking young men, still wearing their army fatigues and shiny high boots, marching every morning for exercise while singing Russian songs. As we marched by, we enjoyed the music and watching the healthy-looking young men.

One evening a few weeks later, the order came that we were to stay in our block and nobody was allowed to leave. All that night the sky was red and smoke belched from the crematorium chimney. By the next morning, we discovered that the thousand young Soviet soldiers had been burned to ashes. These events were supposed to be secret, but we almost always found out what happened the nights we were not allowed to leave our block. We shed tears for the innocent young men and thought of their mothers somewhere in the Soviet Union, who would never find out what happened to their sons since no record of their names would be left behind.

Somehow, we always knew when a holiday was coming. That year for Tisha B'Av, the day we mourn the destruction of our Holy Temple in Jerusalem, we were very determined to maintain the traditional fast as we had been accustomed to doing at home in prior years, even though all the inmates were already half starved.

I was still working with the road-building crew of women, making a path to the nearly finished convalescent home for young Nazi soldiers who were sent there for a few days' rest before returning to the fighting at the front. These young men were so deeply indoctrinated with Hitler's ideals that when they looked at us inmates, they ridiculed our looks as if we were not even human beings. It is true that we didn't look like much. Shorn of our hair and wearing ill-fitting rags, we moved slowly, had only despair in our eyes and wore bleak, miserable faces that spoke of hunger. They felt no pity for us. To them, we were nothing more than freaks who were there to accept punishment for crimes unknown. The teasing and sly remarks by these young men were just extra salt on our wounds, our hurt pride and our misery.

On the eve of Tisha B'Av, when the day's work was finally over, we marched back to our sleeping quarters, singing to help us forget our rumbling, empty stomachs. But before we had a chance to rest, we had to line up for the dreaded *Zählappell*, the counting of heads, which we had to endure for hours, twice daily.

The SS woman who was doing the count was being extremely cruel. She enjoyed her role as a tyrant, venting her own frustrations on us. She counted us over and over again, but her tally just didn't add up. That could only mean that one woman was missing from our line. She became hysterical, threatening us with punishment, abusive words flowing from her enraged lips. But we knew that her counting couldn't be right. Who could be missing, since escape from that hell was practically impossible? After all, we were all locked behind electrified barbed-wire fencing.

As we were standing there, starved and exhausted, we were all thinking of the slice of bread and hot watery soup that would be our evening meal. We looked up at the sky worriedly as the sun disappeared. The eve of Tisha B'Av was almost upon us. After the sun set, we would not be able to eat if we were to keep our vow to fast. But the counting went on and on and our alarm increased as time dragged on.

Fate was against us that night. In the end, nobody was missing from the line. The SS woman had either miscounted or simply took pleasure in inflicting more punishment upon us, knowing that we were helpless in her power. As the first star appeared on the horizon, we became bitterly resigned to the reality that we would have to start fasting on an empty stomach. And that was exactly what we did. As the next day of fasting came to an end, we hoped and prayed that this terrible situation would pass and we would be free again.

~

Annie Lieberman was no older than fifteen and a vivacious, pretty teenager with bright, shining eyes and a sweet disposition. She was undernourished from her long hardship in a concentration camp and emotionally broken from her family's constant fear of being shipped to Auschwitz. Unfortunately, fate didn't spare her family. They were selected for transport and sent to Auschwitz. On arrival, Mr. and Mrs. Lieberman and three of their younger children were sent immediately to the gas chamber. Only Annie was spared and sent to work in one of the labour battalions. But even the hard conditions she had lived through had not dampened her lively spirit.

I met Annie for the first time while we were both making side-walks for the young SS soldiers' convalescent home. As we worked, she often talked about her life before the war, the happy childhood she had had in Belgium, her young parents and family around her. She had a sweet voice and we loved to listen to her singing in French and German. We, the more mature girls in our company, took Annie under our wings immediately and were determined to save her. She was a lovely child, and we all felt compassion and sympathy for one so young and brave. All of us believed that we had a duty to watch out for her.

We finished the road-building project in early September 1944 and were staying in the camp for a few days, waiting for a new assignment. But it was dangerous to be jobless. We knew that anyone who was not working was an easy target for Dr. Mengele and the other selection officers as they made their daily inspections among the workers. Dr. Mengele and his henchmen were cruising all day to catch victims for the crematorium. Without any physical examinations, he selected the ones who would live and those who would die. You didn't have to be sick or weak; if he didn't like your face, that was enough. So we constantly feared for our lives. I can't remember Mengele's face, but his terrifying voice will haunt me forever. When he was in the vicinity, we just froze. Our fear of him was so great.

Even in those terrible conditions, most of us didn't want to end our own lives. Very few people committed suicide — we just wouldn't give our torturers that satisfaction.

My father's advice that I should always try to work was right. We waited anxiously for the next assignment, and luckily an old Wehrmacht soldier of high rank came to the camp one day to recruit twenty women to clean the watchtowers around the crematorium. Annie and I were among those selected. They gave us pink kerchiefs for our shaven heads and we became the "pink commandos." To clean the watchtower windows, we had to fetch water from the nearby creek and were allowed to go there without any guards following us. To get there, we had to cross a clearing that was part of Kanada, where women worked day and night shifts to clear the mountain of clothes, shoes and personal belongings that people had left behind. Since the girls in our *Kommando* unit went back and forth daily, we often smuggled notes and life-saving medicines to people in the camp and became the liaisons between those who worked in other parts of the camp.

Appearances and personal cleanliness were essential in Auschwitz in order to be spared the fate of the crematoria, but we had no opportunity to wash or change clothes. Women prisoners had only one dress, without underwear, and no kerchiefs for their shaven heads. So, women who weren't working often lingered near the gate each morning, waiting for us as we marched to our working place. We quickly exchanged clothes and shoes with them, leaving them our clean clothes and shoes. In the evening, we were back with fresh clothes from the storage depot, to be exchanged again the next morning. The punishment would be severe if we were caught, but we had to help these unfortunate people.

The real danger for us, though, was when we smuggled in medicines to save lives, because we never knew when we might be body-searched. We knew that if we were caught the punishment was certain death, but some of the requests were so vital we could not refuse.

One day, a pretty young woman cornered me with a serious request. She told me that the night before she had given birth to a baby. She begged me to bring some Aspirin for her baby. I was distraught, knowing exactly what she wanted the Aspirin for. I refused but she ran after me crying hysterically, telling me that, if she let the baby live, Mengele would send both the baby and herself to be killed.

"I am young," she sobbed. "I hope my husband will survive and I can have another baby, but if Mengele kills both my baby and me, it is on your conscience."

Her words disturbed me. All day I tortured myself. Should I do it? Should I save the mother or let her die with her child? Could I play God and help her kill an innocent human being? At the end of the day, I did get the Aspirin for her. She waited by the gate and thanked me, crying the whole time. I never found out if she made it and survived that terrible experience. I still have nightmares about the role I played in destroying a human being. I just pray I shall never be tested again.

Cleaning the watchtowers around one of the crematoria was emotionally the hardest job I had to do in Auschwitz. The crematoria were large, low buildings that had no windows, just tall chimneys continuously pouring out black smoke. In order to fetch a pail of water for cleaning the tower windows, we had to pass the fence to get to the nearby creek. As we walked along, we could see tragedy unfolding there, people sitting and waiting for their turn, some perhaps not knowing what their fate would be.

The stench of burning bodies lingered above us all the time. From the windows of the watchtowers, we clearly saw the people walking toward the gas chambers — old and young, mothers with babies in their arms — while vans brought the cripples and the sick. They waited behind the barbed wire for their turn to be led to the place of no return. When a large transport arrived, the overflow of ashes ended up on the burning pyres hidden in what we called the forbidden forest so we could not see.

In the beginning, we tried to deny the truth. But when we spoke to the men who worked inside one of the crematoria where the bodies were turned to ash, ashes which they then spread in large containers, they confirmed our fears. One of the workers was a man who had arrived in the same transport as I had. His name was Elek Horivitz, and he had married a lovely girl named Ellie just a month before. Ellie now slept in the same barracks as my friends and I did. Once, we even smuggled her out in our *Kommando* unit so she could see her husband behind the fence. Without a word, they waved at each other and said goodbye.

The yard in front of the gas chamber building was well maintained, with flower beds and other greenery to disguise the real purpose of the buildings and to pacify the crying, hungry and exhausted children while they waited. As we cleaned the windows and floors in the watchtowers, we saw the children through the windows, playing outside the crematorium with no idea of what would happen to them in a short time. We, in the tower, silently said goodbye to them, crying as we watched them going with their parents down the stairs on a journey from which there would be no return. A few hours later, the sky would turn red, belching out smoke from the chimney and filling the air with the smell of burning bodies.

A few teenage boys were assigned to take care of the flowers in front of the gas chamber building and were forbidden to talk to the people there awaiting their fates. But these boys were in a terrible state of mind, heartbroken and very lonely. As we passed by the fence one day, a young man named Marek approached the fence and, seeing Annie, threw over a package for her. When she opened the hand-kerchief, there was a piece of bread and a little bundle of sugar in it.

Annie was surprised and happy with the extra nourishment and was looking forward to seeing Marek again the next morning. Sure enough, there he was the next day, waiting by the fence with a little package. We all noticed the smile on Annie's face. She was full of ex-citement and after a few short weeks Annie was in love. She could talk of nothing else but Marek and the hope of freedom to come. The extra portion of bread helped too, and Annie slowly regained her strength.

Their love blossomed without their even being able to touch each other's hands. Even with the electric fence between them, theirs was a pure and trusting love. Annie endured the cold and hardship in the hope that all would end soon and she would be with Marek ever after.

But fate was not kind to them.

~

Like many others, I had become a walking zombie in Auschwitz-Birkenau. The bestial treatment by the SS soldiers, the constant hun-ger, the hard work and the realization that my whole family had been killed made every day a horror.

In the late fall of 1944, I was still part of the *Kommando* team cleaning watchtowers around one of the crematoria. On quiet days, when the activities in this crematorium were slowed down, we dared to leave the towers after finishing our jobs to pick blackberries on the edge of the forbidden forest. If we were lucky enough to pick a dish full of berries and smuggle it back into the camp, we would sell it for a loaf of bread. At that time, a loaf of bread was considered the ultimate luxury.

One day, as we emerged from the forest after picking berries, the commandant of the crematorium noticed us and ordered us to hand our berries over to him. Before we had a chance to think about the terrible situation we were in, a soldier was behind us ordering us back to the camp site. Confused and frightened, we marched into the camp.

Once inside, we stood in the middle of the square for a long time while the Germans gathered all the information about us and discussed our fate. The verdict was that we had wanted to run away and the punishment for that crime was public hanging. They even decided that the time of the execution would be 10 o'clock the next morning. The entire camp population was forced to watch these hangings, the horrible consequence for those who tried to escape.

Of the five of us, two had sisters who were not involved in this terrible incident. The sisters became hysterical and started to run around asking for advice to see if anything could be done. Nobody had an answer. Since there was no trial, there could be no defence presented. The Germans did as they pleased with us.

Late that night, one of our supervisors advised us to go over to the next barracks to speak with a Jewish commandant named Ethel, who had the reputation of being a good soul. Although she had been there a very long time, she hadn't lost her compassion and sympathy for the less fortunate. She was responsible for a thousand women and she tried to be humane.

When we arrived, she had just lit the Sabbath candle in her little cubicle. She had heard about our misfortune and gently told us what we already knew — there was no way out of our terrible situation. She prayed with us and blessed us and wished us a peaceful journey. Numb in body and soul, we walked back to our sleeping quarters. That night was the longest of my life. Early the next morning, a young girl arrived with a message from Ethel. She had found a connection to the commandant who handled our case. For five gold watches, our lives could be spared. The watches were found in Kanada and the sentence was terminated with a warning that we should never dare to visit the forest again.

We found out later that the German commandant, an elderly man who smuggled liquor out to the workers in the crematorium in return for gold, diamonds and other valuables in a bulging attaché case, thought the higher-ups might ask him where he was while we were wandering around. He pulled a few strings in order to save himself. Ethel saved our lives.

~

One day in the beginning of October 1944, we were in the watch-tower and had finished our cleaning work early. It happened to be the sixth day of Sukkot, and we were praying with bitter hearts to the Almighty for a miracle to be free again. Startled by a sudden big noise, we looked out the window to see an inmate hanging on the electric fence. He had thrown himself on the fence to destroy it. A few minutes later, there was a loud explosion from Crematorium 4, followed by fire and yelling and shooting. Frightened, we fell on the ground and hid our faces, wondering what was going on. The Auschwitz uprising had begun.

SS men were running around and shooting at everyone who moved and some charged into the tower and found five frightened girls lying on the floor. They ordered us to go down to join the girls from the other tower, which we did. When we reached the main gate, our guard reported to his supervisor that he had found us in the tower. "These Kommandos know too much," the supervisor told the guard. "They have to go." Instantly, we knew they were going to kill us. Feeling destiny had a different plan in store for us.

Miraculously, instead of being killed, we were part of a group of a thousand women who were put on a train out of Auschwitz. After a few days of travel, we arrived at another concentration camp in Germany called Ravensbrück.

We later met others from Auschwitz who told us that, a day after the uprising, a long train arrived from Germany with its human cargo. Because of the chaos at the camp with Crematorium 4 having been burned down during the uprising, the Nazis left unfortunate people dying of thirst and hunger in the closed cattle cars. The people who told us the story said they heard these poor souls in the train cars crying and begging for mercy. Eventually, the train was reversed and sent to Ravensbrück.

When we were there the facilities were even worse than the conditions in Auschwitz. The Germans put us in quarantine for three weeks when we arrived, so we weren't working. It was winter, freezing cold and there was no hope. Since there was nothing else to do, when the *Appells* were over in the mornings we just lay on our beds dreaming about food and freedom.

Lice started to spread because of the filth. Just one louse bit me and I scratched it, which left a visible red spot on the pale white skin of my stomach. The following day, or the day after, when the quarantine was almost over, we were taken for an examination so that they could select workers. They immediately pushed me out of line because I had that spot on my stomach. I knew this could be the end for me, but I had no more tears left to cry about my fate. I was certain that I would never come out alive from Ravensbrück.

My friend Annie was sent with us out of Auschwitz. We found out that Annie's love, Marek, had been killed in the uprising in the crematorium. When Annie found out about Marek, she lost the will to live. We tried to talk some sense into her, but her heart was broken and nothing mattered to her anymore. She did her work automatically, answered when we tried to cheer her up, but she was depressed, no longer that cheerful child.

Another miracle happened to me in Ravensbrück. When I was pushed out of the workers' line my friends — there were five of us who were always together — were all distraught, but one of them, an especially lively girl, had heard about someone who might help us, a Hungarian girl whom Mengele had done experiments on in the hospital. He had injected her with male hormones, causing her to grow a long black beard and to develop a man's deep voice. That woman was very bitter and full of hate, yet somehow my friend contacted her and asked her for a favour.

"What will you give me for it?" the bearded woman asked my friend.

"What do you want?"

"I need a good pair of shoes."

My friend came back to me and said, "Judy, take off your shoes."

I happened to have a good pair of shoes because we were dressed a little better there than we had been in Auschwitz. My friend's sister had a good apron and another girl had a sweater, so we pooled everything we had together, and my friend went back and gave it all to the woman.

The woman took the parcel and said, "Tell your friend to be at the Appell tomorrow morning at 6 o'clock when they call names for this group."

I didn't sleep all night. I couldn't believe that it could happen and I would be saved. But my friends dragged me with them to the *Appell* wearing this woman's old shoes. At the *Appell*, they called names in alphabetical order. One of my friends' last name was Altman and my other friend's name was Gross, so they were called early. Since my name was Schwarcz, I had to wait until nearly the end of the alphabet to see if I would be called. When they finally called my name, I felt so relieved that I promised myself that I would never complain again. Whatever would be, I would try to make the best of it.

I was part of a group of a thousand women who were shipped to a camp outside the town of Malchow in northern Germany to work in a munitions factory there, where we made bullets for light artillery. The work in Malchow was tedious and needed real concentration since we had to weigh the gunpowder exactly, press it into the bullet and then polish it to perfection. Twenty young women on the assembly line would work in unison. We sang to keep awake, especially when we worked the twelve-hour-long night shifts without a break.

One friend of mine kept track of the passing months by marking the days on her upper leg with a small piece of pencil. As a result, we always knew when *Rosh Chodesh*, the new month, arrived. In November 1944, I had been a prisoner in Nazi concentration camps for six months, and as the month of Kislev neared, we knew that Chanukah would soon arrive. We were heartbroken because we had no way to celebrate the Festival of Lights in our totally darkened existence. Hunger and lack of proper winter clothes had already taken their toll on our spirits, but how could we not remember Chanukah? We decided that, no matter what, we would celebrate the holiday. We still had a spark of hope left and prayed that another miracle would happen.

We started to save our tiny portions of margarine. We pulled some thread from a blanket and rolled it into a wick. The eldest girl among us started to prepare the lighting of our makeshift Chanukah candle while two girls watched by the door for any sudden appearance of the Nazis. We knew the danger of being caught as we melted the margarine in a dish and fixed the wick. Now we were ready for the ceremony. We sang the blessings of the lights in unison, tears rolling down our cheeks, as the little flickering light gave us hope for a better tomorrow.

# Liberation

It was in Malchow that I met my cousin Regina (Rivkah) Lebensfeld. I had heard that she was in Auschwitz when I was there, but we did not meet because she was working in a different area of the camp. Someone told me Regina was also in Malchow and took me to see her. I encountered a sweet face, a face that was just the same as my grandfather's, so I felt right away that she was family.

"Who are you?" she asked me in German, her only language, and when I explained our connection, we hugged. It felt wonderful to have found a cousin. Regina was deeply compassionate and always watched out for me, and we remained very close.

Another woman who made it to Malchow with us was Emilia. Emilia was a dark-haired, beautiful woman with dimples on her always-smiling face. Shining black eyes with long lashes dominated her features. She came from a middle-class, assimilated Jewish family in Czechoslovakia and was married to a gentile who had had a high-ranking position in the government. They had four sons and were a very close-knit family with a happy, financially secure home life befitting the social rank of a civil servant.

Regardless of her husband's position, Emilia had been picked up by the Gestapo and sent to Auschwitz. I first met her in Ravensbrück, and then in Malchow we worked in the same unit in the munitions factory. She couldn't have been more than thirty-six years old then, but by German standards she was considered an old woman already. Knowing what happened to "old people," she tried to take care of herself and prove that she could still do the harsh work assigned to us.

She was always cheerful, helping others and offering a shoulder to cry on. After finishing our long and tedious day of work, mostly in night shifts, we had a few hours to rest and that was when she would tell us about her loving husband and about her life in her beloved Prague before the war.

In early 1945, the war came close to the camouflaged munitions factory in the forest where we worked. American airplanes now constantly flew overhead, dropping bombs over the forest where the war production was conducted, trying to destroy the munitions factories. The Nazis continued to pretend that all was going well, but when the air-raid sirens started to sound, the German supervisor and the SS guards ran down to the shelter, leaving us abandoned in the darkened factory.

Even in those nerve-wracking days and nights, the Nazis had one-track minds, always consumed with how to torture the overworked, underfed, desperate pile of human beings in their charge. One day, Emilia was called to the commandant's office. The poor thing was very frightened and wondered what they would do to her. We all held our breath, waiting anxiously for her return to the barracks.

She finally returned, crying hysterically, and told us what the Nazis had requested. They wanted her to sign a document saying that she would divorce her husband. They told her that if she refused, they would send her sons to the gas chamber and her husband to a forced labour camp. She had no alternative but to sign. We tried to console her by saying that, if she survived, her husband would understand that the paper had been signed under force and would certainly take her back. But she cried all the time, praying that she would see her family again.

By the second half of April 1945, after months of labouring in this camp, we knew the war was finally coming to an end and fervently hoped and prayed we would survive. American bombers continued to frequently fly over the bunker, and by that time the factory where we worked had already been closed for two weeks. Our misery grew as more inmates were brought in from other camps, our starvation rations were again cut in half and we were forced to sleep in sitting positions due to lack of space. I had the good fortune to find work repairing and sewing civilian clothes for the SS women in the sewing room where it was warm.

On the first of May, the Nazis organized long columns of women, opened the gate and started marching us from our camp toward the town of Malchow. We didn't know where we were going — we were now out in the unknown.

One thousand hungry, tired women marched through the night, five to a row, herded by armed SS guards on bicycles. The weather was still chilly, especially when it rained and we got soaked through and through. The only sustenance we had was the rain we caught by opening our mouths. Our energy was ebbing away, but we kept going. I lost track of women I knew during this march, including Emilia.

We were allowed to rest in a muddy field for a couple of hours early one morning before resuming our march toward a town called Goldberg. By the afternoon, we noticed that our tormentors had started disappearing, one by one, and we found ourselves abandoned. As we walked along, we saw that the ditches along the road were filled with medals, insignias and guns that had been left behind by the cowardly SS guards who had dropped all evidence of their military status and exchanged their uniforms for civilian clothes.

The road was crowded with German civilians, which made it very difficult to move. Besides, we were afraid they might harm us. We debated whether we should try to hide but decided to keep moving. Since we had red marks painted on the backs of our coats and the sleeves were a different colour, it was very obvious from the way we looked that we were inmates from a camp.

When we reached a small village, we decided it was time to find a place to hide. By that time, there were only ten of us together, including my cousin Regina. We had lost touch with all the other women. In the village, we found that the German population had left in haste, knowing that the Soviet army was just kilometres away. We found a barn with an open door and a ladder leading up to the loft, so we snuck up, burrowed into the hay and made ourselves invisible. Although our bodies were totally exhausted, we couldn't sleep because our hunger was so great.

We later heard men talking in French in the yard below and smelled the heavenly aroma of fresh coffee. Regina courageously went to investigate. A few minutes later, she came back and excitedly told us that the men were escaped French prisoners of war who had raided a German military food depot and had brought a whole carriage of food with them. After finding out who we were, they invited us to share their food. One by one, we came down and were welcomed with a cup of coffee and a large slice of bread spread with margarine.

Their group consisted of nineteen young men. They had information that the Americans were not far away, and even though they were also exhausted, they planned to walk all night to reach them. They warned us to leave the barn because the Soviet army was close and would surely occupy the village by morning. We knew that the Soviet army was dangerous and their treatment of women was brutal. They offered to protect and feed us if we would help pull the food wagon, so we decided to continue our journey in their company.

We trudged all night along a road through the human chaos. The road was crowded with tanks carrying German soldiers and exploding bombs occasionally lit up the rainy darkness. Early in the morning of May 3, 1945, we stopped at a farmhouse near Schwerin and asked permission to rest in the barn. The good farmer agreed but refused to allow the men and women to sleep under the same roof. The men were allowed to sleep in the stable but the ten women had to sleep in the open field. Our new friends made a makeshift tent for us to protect us a little from the cold.

The next morning, after a cup of hot coffee and bread, we continued our journey toward freedom. As we were walking, one of the Frenchmen caught a chicken with a string, so we stopped and made a fire and had the first cup of chicken soup we had tasted in more than a year. We kept walking, but by the afternoon, we were all totally exhausted. We sat down by the forest's edge and decided not to go any further. My shoes were in tatters, and I was walking barefoot on the frozen ground, so my feet were full of blisters.

As I sat nursing my sore feet, a loud yell drew my attention toward the main road and then a loud noise made us jump. Peeking out from behind the forest cover, we saw the first American tank with its star-spangled banner proudly waving and young soldiers sitting inside. Suddenly, the forest came alive as refugees who had been hiding there ran out shouting to kiss the boots of the shocked soldiers. We must have really frightened them, because we looked like we were from another planet. A few of them spoke German and advised us to stay put as the Red Cross would pick us up the next day.

Our gallant French companions decided to continue their journey and we decided to stay overnight in a nearby stable. The owners were rude and wouldn't let us in, but by morning the owners had disappeared, leaving the doors wide open, and we settled down in an attic. We helped ourselves to some food that morning and eventually started out again on the road to meet the liberating American army. People were running in all directions, and although we were physically exhausted, our spirits soared because we knew we were free at last.

On May 5, we met some former inmates, driving an abandoned German truck, who took us to Schwerin where the Red Cross lodged us in a former Nazi headquarters. They took the sick ones to the overcrowded hospitals and fed the rest of us. But the first decent food provided by our American liberators inadvertently caused much sickness and death. Our emaciated bodies simply could not digest the food that was given to us so generously by the kind-hearted soldiers. The hospitals filled up with former camp inmates whose stomachs had succumbed to the sudden overeating after a long period of starvation. In addition, typhus and many other contagious diseases were ravaging our weary bodies.

Though many of us got better physically, the slowest healing was psychological. It took a long time for us to be able to enjoy the freedom of walking on the streets without the feeling of being watched by the hated Nazi guards. We were simply grateful to be alive, yet it was difficult to absorb the implications of our unexpected new reality.

I was sad that Annie, who had once been so joyous when she found love in Auschwitz, was not with us. On the last working day in the factory before liberation, we had been separated from Annie. She was liberated by the Soviet army instead of the American side. Some of my friends who were with her later told me about what happened after liberation. Annie stayed on in Germany because she had nowhere else to go. She became very ill with tuberculosis and died in the hospital. She had given up hope and didn't want to live anymore after losing so much, especially the man she loved.

We were determined, however, to celebrate our liberation, which meant commemorating the joyous Jewish holiday of Shavuot on May 18 and 19. Regina decided to light holiday candles, but in the midst of our celebration we heard loud banging at the door. We cautiously opened the door to three American soldiers, who were very agitated and scolded us in German for lighting candles since a blackout was still in effect and our light had been noticed by the American patrols.

When Regina explained that we were Jews and the candles had been lit in honour of the Shavuot holiday, two of the soldiers at the door started to cry as they looked at us with unbelieving joy. They said they were Jewish themselves and we were the first Jews they had seen and were so happy to find us. With tears still running down their cheeks, they hugged us and asked many questions about our miraculous liberation.

Early the next morning, our new friends arrived in an American truck with another Jewish fellow, a doctor who wanted to make sure we were all right. They took us to a very nice villa where the couple who owned the house were welcoming and apologized, telling us that they had never heard of a concentration camp. Our American friends, Mr. Cooper and Mr. Saafeld, visited us every day there, bringing food from their own army rations. We were always hungry and appreciated their kindness but we had to be careful since our weak stomachs couldn't tolerate the sudden abundance.

Our friends also brought an old sewing machine and some bed sheets from an SS barracks, and I worked overtime to sew dresses for us so we could look presentable. The blue-and-white checkered bed sheets made lovely dresses. These two Americans became our mentors and adoptive fathers, slowly restoring our faith and dignity and helping us celebrate our deliverance from our enemies. Their simple human decency helped to heal our deep emotional wounds and gave us the hope we needed to continue with our lives. We started to gain weight quickly and our hair started to grow back. We began to look like human beings again.

One night, some drunken American soldiers banged on the gate, wanting to socialize with the former camp inmates they heard were living in the house. Our terrified landlord begged us to let them in but, of course, we didn't. The next morning, we went to the American headquarters to complain about the harassment. The Americans provided us with a guard every night by the gate so we could sleep in peace.

To our great sorrow, the American army left after six weeks, and we had to say goodbye to our mentors. With tears and promises to keep in touch, they provided us with a car, some food and a record player with two records, which we played constantly. Even today, I get nostalgic when I hear those soothing melodies from long ago.

After the Americans left, the British military transferred us to the town of Lüneburg, where we stayed in an army barracks. The food there was hardly edible and we had to find ways to improve it. Our American friends had found a sack of salt in an abandoned house, which they gave us. This was a treasure since salt was used as a currency then, and we bartered the salt with the cook for some food. He was happy to oblige but, that day, the whole camp came down with diarrhea because our precious sack of salt turned out to be inedible Epsom salt. The cook was very angry with us and we didn't dare show ourselves for the next few days.

Our days in Lüneburg were filled with restlessness and uncertainty since we were mentally preparing for the trip to our former homes and wondering what we might find when we got there. We were jumpy and anxious, fearful of the unknown. Our return to freedom had overwhelmed us with uncertainty. Where would we go? What would we find? Was it possible to heal the unbearable pain and suffering that had reduced us to breathing shells, broken in spirit and body?

After six weeks in Lüneburg, the Slovakian government sent a few buses to bring their citizens home. Among the ten girls in our group, most were from Bratislava. I was the only Hungarian and I didn't speak the Slovak language, but Regina decided that I had to go with her in the bus regardless of my citizenship and our inability to speak the language. She covered my face with a kerchief and I pretended that I had a very bad toothache and couldn't talk. That solved my speaking problem and I kept quiet the whole trip.

After a few days, we arrived in Prague, where people welcomed us as if we were heroes back from the war. The Red Cross took care of us for a few days, but we wanted to go on. With heavy hearts, we boarded the overloaded train to our next destination, Bratislava. The train was so full there was no room to sit down, not even on the floor, so we stood for the entire day. We finally arrived at the railway station in Bratislava, which was soon filled with Soviet soldiers, excited civilians and a cacophony of noise.

It was late in the evening and we were tired, hungry and unsure of what to do next. Out of nowhere, an old acquaintance of Regina's appeared, a Jewish man who welcomed us warmly. He told Margit, one of the girls in our group, that he knew for sure that her mother, Mrs. Singer, was still alive and living in a basement on the Judengasse, Jewish street, in the old Jewish quarter. It sounded incredible to us that the old woman could still be alive since we knew what happened to the elderly in Auschwitz. Margit started to cry and she and Regina decided to go into town to investigate while the rest of us sat down on our meagre baggage and waited.

After what felt like an eternity, they returned with the news that, yes, the old woman was alive but frail and bedridden. The Nazis believed she would not survive the transport to Auschwitz and had left her behind. The Jewish underground sent her some food, and by sheer determination she kept herself alive for the sole purpose of seeing the day of her daughter's return. She had even kept all of Margit's clothes clean and waiting for her return. We walked back to her place and were greeted by this special woman. We arrived in Bratislava on a Thursday evening and spent the Sabbath with Mrs. Singer. Unfortunately, the old woman's happiness at seeing her only surviving child was too much for her. Her weak heart couldn't take the excitement, and two weeks later she passed away. But she died with peace in her heart.

That Saturday night a train was leaving for Budapest, and I decided to try to get home to Hungary. Despite my cousin begging me to stay with her for a while, I was restless and determined to find out what had happened to my family.

# As an Unwanted Stranger

Only when I returned from the forced labour camp did I understand how thoroughly the war had devastated the world I had known. When I arrived in the town where I had spent my early life, I felt like an unwanted stranger. Even the streets looked different, with unfriendly neighbours and former acquaintances staring at me as if they were seeing a ghost from another world. Our former neighbours were apologetic and obviously disturbed by my sudden reappearance. In their minds, they had already buried all the Jews.

Szerencs, the city where I had been raised and had lived almost all my life, had suddenly become a strange, repellent place, full of sad memories. With a wildly beating heart and shaking legs, I knocked on the door to our house. My brother Yitzhak opened the door and we fell into each other's arms, crying hysterically. Our house was occupied by strangers and the furniture and everything else that had once belonged to us had disappeared. These curious people whom I didn't know, also survivors, looked at us and felt our pain.

Yitzhak and I had many questions for each other and, unfortunately, we soon realized the sad truth that we were the sole survivors of our entire family. Yitzhak was the only one of my brothers to survive, after his own long struggle. Within a month of the Nazi occupation of Hungary, the order had come from the government that all Jews had to wear the yellow star. Just over a month after that order, around the time we were shipped to Auschwitz-Birkenau, Yitzhak had been called into the Jewish labour force to dig ditches for the fighting Hungarian army on the Soviet front. When the war was almost over, as the Nazis and their Hungarian collaborators lost their power, they took the Jewish brigade with them and shipped them to Germany's concentration camps to be killed. My brother and many others were jammed into cattle cars that were scheduled to leave Hungary by morning light. But Yitzhak was determined not to let them go to their certain doom. During the night, he started to unscrew the boards on the floor and managed to squeeze himself out, followed by a friend. As they were fleeing, the Nazis shot at them and one bullet hit his friend. Yitzhak tore the yellow star from his jacket and put on a Red Cross armband that he had hidden in his clothes. He picked up his injured friend and carried him to the nearest hospital in the dark of night.

Yitzhak finally reached Budapest but didn't know where he might find shelter until he arrived at the Swiss consulate. But the doorman told him they were overwhelmed with refugees and had no room left. While he was debating with the man about where he should hide, a large delivery truck arrived with bread, and Yitzhak grabbed a large bag, flung it over his shoulder and walked right in through the open gate. Once inside, he mingled with those inside and then stayed.

After Hungary's liberation by the Soviet army in 1945, Yitzhak went back to our home to wait for our family to return. He wandered alone in our former hometown, unable to find peace of mind. One day, in a pile of garbage, he found our father's insurance contract with the bank showing his many monthly payments on my behalf. He took the deed to the head office in Budapest and was offered a ridiculously small amount compared to what they owed. He was so angry he tore the contract to pieces and threw it into the garbage.

Unfortunately, I was the only one from our family Yitzhak would ever welcome back from the war. My maternal grandparents were in their early eighties when they were transported, along with all our uncles, aunts and their families, to be killed in Auschwitz. No trace is left of them. They live only in the memories of their few surviving grandchildren. After the war, I attempted to visit the grave of my paternal grandfather, who had died before the war, but even his tombstone had disappeared, and I could not find his resting place. However, his memory and the memory of the rest of my family lives in my heart for as long as I am alive.

Flora, who my mother had met when she visited Yitzhak in Budapest years earlier, had arrived back home to Slovakia and had sent Yitzhak a telegram to let him know that she was alive and well. I insisted that he go to look for her.

Yitzhak left Hungary, and another thirteen years would pass before I saw him again. He did marry Flora, and they ended up in France, where they became the guardians of 150 young orphans. Flora and Yitzhak were helping to take care of these children at a temporary facility, working on behalf of the Bnei Akiva religious Zionist youth movement. They then left for Israel in May 1948, when Israel became a state. Yitzhak was called up for army service soon after they arrived and fought with the tanks unit, the armoured corps. Flora, meanwhile, worked in a hospital taking care of wounded soldiers.

Yitzhak and Flora lived in a one-room house and life was hard at first. But soon they became proud parents of a little girl, Rachel, named after our mother. Yitzhak became a very proud Israeli who fought in both the 1948 War of Independence and the 1956 Suez campaign. He felt that finally he had arrived home. When he died of cancer in 2003, I was in Israel and I saw him a few days before his death.

When Yitzhak left to look for Flora, I spent the first night in my parents' bedroom crying, looking at the few pieces of furniture left from our former life. I felt that even the house was crying with me. I couldn't sleep and I knew I couldn't stay in that house. I knew that my younger brother, Shimon, sixteen at the time of our deportation, had buried a tin box that held our family heirlooms, including my father's golden watch and chain, my mother's rings and diamond earrings and other valuables. Unfortunately, I had no idea where he had put the box and had no desire to look for it. That part of my life was gone forever, jewellery and furniture included. Most likely the box is still buried somewhere in the yard behind our house.

The final blow hit me when I saw a woman walking toward me on the main street wearing my mother's best dress. I just stared at her, stunned and speechless, the tears running down my cheeks. That did it. As if someone were chasing me, I ran back to the railway station, never to return.

~

In Hungary, especially in the smaller towns, modern ideas about women's liberation didn't exist. My mother, grandmother and great-grandma before them had only one mission in life: to take care of their husbands and children and to carry out their household duties as well as doing some kind of social and charity work. This filled their lives and they did their duties without any complaint or resentment. It was simply natural and expected that I, my parents' only daughter, would follow in the footsteps of my beloved ancestors.

But the war disrupted this tradition and these expectations. After being liberated from the concentration camps, I found myself hope-lessly alone without any guidance from anyone. How, given my previous sheltered existence, could I put my life together to face the world alone? This was the problem.

There was one thing I knew for sure: I couldn't build a new life on the old ashes. The city where I was raised had become a strange place. Nobody seemed to care if I was dead or alive. After a few miserable days, I had run away from the painful memories of our birthplace. I chose immigration to pre-state Israel, the land of our forefathers, to be with my own kind.

While I waited to be accepted by the immigration committee, winter set in and all activities ceased till the spring, when the Danube River would be navigable again. After I realized I had no home to return to, I discovered that one of my mother's brothers, Uncle Willy, had survived, and he invited me to stay with him for the winter in Mezőkövesd. During the long winter, I found shelter with my uncle, who had lost his wife and needed medical attention and loving care. He was alone and I kept house for him.

His house stood just around the corner from my paternal grandparents' home, and on the way to the market I had to pass the old house where my grandparents, the Schwarczes, had once lived and which had been the scene of many happy family memories. The first time I went by that house on the way to the market, I had the shock of my life. The house, that beautiful house of my childhood, where I would visit and play in the summers, was in ruins. It had no roof, windows or doors; even the wooden floors were missing. Completely abandoned, it stared at me like a big question mark. What had happened? Where was everybody? I stood there paralyzed, rubbing my eyes and waiting to wake up from this bad dream.

As my eyes wandered through the open holes where the windows had once been, I noticed my treasured chair, mutilated, with its covers cut to shreds, the buttons and one leg missing. It was a discarded, lonely witness to our tragedy. Finally, after six weeks of uncertainty and worry about my family's fate, I had to face, in my despair, what I had suspected all along. Of my beloved family, only my brother Yitzhak had survived. All my pent-up emotions broke loose at that moment and I cried bitterly over the memories of summers gone by and the loss of my previous life and family.

Fate, however, was about to intervene. In early 1946, at my uncle's, I met Béla, my future husband, who, with his surviving brothers and nieces, was planning to emigrate to Palestine. A few months later, Béla and I left Hungary with a group of young people. The goal was to settle in the Land of Israel. Unfortunately, the British blockade prevented us, the broken-hearted survivors, from entering the land of our forefathers, and we were sent instead to a Displaced Persons (DP) camp in Italy.

# Free to Wait

Béla and I, along with a few of his relatives, arrived in Grugliasco, Italy, near Turin, in April 1946. The town sanatorium was handed over to the refugees for a few years and it became a DP camp and transit camp for people waiting for visas to emigrate somewhere. Many of the young, single people risked the dangerous journey to Palestine. Unfortunately, most were stopped by the British and ended up in detention camps in Cyprus. Little by little, though, they were released and eventually settled in Israel after the United Nations voted to establish a homeland for the Jews in May 1948.

I worked in the clothing depot to help the people who arrived from Poland, Siberia and all over Europe, many having survived in the ghettos and concentration camps for six years. For many, broken in body and spirit, the stay in Grugliasco helped to heal their physical wounds, aid their spiritual recovery and facilitate their common wish to rejoin the human race.

UNRRA camp number 17 was well organized and under British supervision. If the management had any idea about the clandestine departures in the middle of the night for the port of Genoa and the waiting ships for Palestine, they didn't show it. They were very proper and polite. We had a doctor's office on the premises to take care of minor illnesses and a steady ambulance service was available for more serious cases. The camp was childless at the beginning — due to the Nazis' murderous policies, most children had not survived the war —

but there were women who were pregnant and the camp slowly filled up with newborns, who brought with them laughter and hope for a brighter future.

I had the honour to be elected vice-president of WIZO Hadassah Women's Zionist Organization in the camp, and my task was to visit the new mothers and supervise teaching them how to handle their infants. The young women had no idea what to do with their helpless babies. Many years of inhumane conditions in the Nazi camps and in Siberia had robbed them of all their common sense, and they had to be re-educated to be able to live in a normal society.

Life was hard in the DP camp, where we were dependent on the generosity of the UNRRA, the United Nations Relief and Rehabilitation Administration, for our daily needs. We were restless, ready to settle down far from war-ravaged Europe and start a new life in a new country. We were now free, but we were waiting to move on with our life. The Italian population was very friendly and sympathetic. We worked out a good relationship with them as we mastered their language.

Since I was a trained dressmaker, I got a job teaching women the elementary skills of how to sew a simple dress. Most of my students were survivors who had little education, since they had spent most of their young lives in ghettos, concentration camps or gulags. The ORT, the Organization for Rehabilitation through Training, a retraining program with headquarters in Switzerland, sent the necessary tools (sewing machines, instruction books, materials) to start a school. I had thirty-nine women who came daily, eager to learn. The only obstacle we had was the language barrier. They all spoke Yiddish but understanding the variations among different dialects was hard for me. Although I had learned a little Yiddish from our neighbours, the dialects from various parts of Poland, Galicia and Romania threw me off. It took me a long time to be able to converse comfortably, and even my knowledge of German, which is similar to Yiddish, was not much help. But somehow we worked through this barrier.

There was great excitement when the women I worked with made their first skirts and, slowly, learned the finer points of sewing. They gained self-confidence in their work and I enjoyed watching their progress as, little by little, they put a dress together and were very pleased with their achievements. I often wonder what happened to my students. I hope their new skills helped them overcome the rough challenges of being a new immigrant somewhere.

As Béla and I prepared for a simple marriage in the Italian DP camp, both of us admitted feeling a strange sort of guilt. How could we celebrate? The war had ended just over a year earlier and it had robbed us of our dearest loved ones. My future husband had lost his first wife and two small children in the war. I was an orphan too, with no relatives to give me away. Our upcoming wedding day was supposed to be the happiest day of our lives. That was the day Béla and I were to start a new life together and live happily ever after. But it was a very solemn day for both of us. We were missing our parents, grandparents, brothers and sisters.

We had become engaged in Hungary and had hoped for a wedding in Palestine among our own people in the land of our forefathers. Unfortunately, we had our dreams and the British had other ideas. Since the British blockade kept the remnants of our people from arriving in the Land of Israel, landing us in Italy instead, we were now living in a strange country in transition. We were simply waiting for permission to travel to and settle in British Mandate Palestine.

Since we still wanted to get married, we approached the rabbi who indicated he would be more than happy to officiate and we set the date — June 9, 1947. As we had no means to make a lavish wedding, we settled on a garden ceremony with a thousand of our new friends, the other homeless refugees in the camp, to share in the happy occasion. No invitations were needed. The whole camp joined in the festivities. Being so poor didn't dampen our spirits or our happiness though. We were grateful just to be alive.

My wedding gown consisted of a second-hand beige suit with a white blouse I had made from a discarded man's shirt. A green silk scarf substituted for the traditional veil. I had washed my new and only white shirt the night before to have it clean and fresh, and my future sister-in-law generously offered to do the ironing. Early in the morning, she went down to the community kitchen for hot coal for the iron and, in her eagerness to please me, she didn't check the iron and burned the collar of my precious blouse. It took a lot of self-control on my part not to be upset by this mishap.

The day of our wedding was beautiful and sunny, the flowers were in bloom and birds were singing. The chuppah consisted of a prayer shawl set on poles in the large garden. A few daring young men climbed over the fence to a neighbouring garden, helped themselves to the abundance of flowers and presented me with a lovely bouquet.

After the ceremony, everybody fetched their own food in the kitchen and joined us for the festive meal consisting of sardines bought by Béla. After the meal, someone played a lively tune on the harmonica and hora dancing started in high spirits and lasted the whole afternoon. We didn't expect or get any wedding presents but we didn't care about that. We were filled with high hopes for a bright future.

The day after the wedding, being an industrious and dutiful wife, I decided to fill our mattresses with fresh straw, so I took them down to the yard where the straw was stacked up high. As I removed the old straw and refilled the mattresses, I didn't notice that my brand new wedding ring had slipped off my finger. As I took the mattresses back, satisfied with the result of my labour, it suddenly dawned on me that my ring was gone. In a panic, I searched everywhere but it never turned up. I was very upset and Béla couldn't console me. He went into the city and bought me an identical ring but this new ring never had the same meaning to me. Interestingly, over the years I thought I lost it many times but I always found it when I was not looking for it.

～

One of my friends in the DP camp was Béla Zimmerman, whom I had met up with again after liberation. The few boys and girls who had returned to Szerencs were orphans in every sense of the word. Béla had become our anchor, and the wise guide who tried to help ease the pain. With his soothing words and friendly approach, he was our father figure, dispensing advice and comfort to those who didn't know which direction to take or how to mend their broken lives.

Within a year, we became elated when Béla Zimmerman married Magdi, the daughter of my husband's sister Leah, who had become my friend in Auschwitz; through both of our marriages, Béla and I were now truly family. He was unable to immigrate with us to Canada, but moved with his wife to Israel.

It was only later that I heard about the good deeds Béla had performed in the Ukraine during the war. He himself was too modest to talk about it, but his friends praised his warm heart and selflessness. He unhesitatingly risked his own life to guide refugees through the forest, giving them money and directions to try to reach Hungary. Béla is no longer with us but he will always be in our hearts. He was a prince of a man among the righteous ones.

~

The camp was overcrowded and people were constantly coming and going as we waited for our turn to leave. The living conditions were far from ideal and the lack of privacy bothered me terribly. To keep busy and make some money, I started to work in the clothing *magazine*, as we called the store. Organizing the files and helping to give out clothes to the needy, I met many people, shared their problems and was often required to use my limited English.

A sweet young woman with two little babies often came in to ask for some clothes for the little ones. She was married to a middle-aged man, both of them for the second time, and they seemed to be happy together. One day, her first husband arrived in the camp and reclaimed her as his wife. She became hysterical, finding out that her first love, to whom she had been married only a short time before the Nazis separated them, was still alive.

She had to make her choice. The second husband, who was the father of the little girls, was very upset, of course, but he had no choice but to let her go. Two weeks later, she was back. The long separation had made her and her first husband strangers, and she felt guilty and miserable for leaving the father of her children. They resumed an almost normal life but now there was a sting in her heart.

Another woman, Mrs. Guttman, used to come in to be consoled, or rather, to have someone lend a sympathetic ear to her wartime story. Because their Hungarian citizenship papers had not been in order, her whole family had been taken to Poland by the Hungarian police and thrown to the mercy of the occupying Nazi forces. Somehow, they had managed to smuggle themselves back to Hungary only to be gunned down by the Hungarian Nazi collaborators. Except for Mrs. Guttman and one young daughter, the whole family of six had been killed. She sent her child ahead to pre-state Israel with the understanding that she would follow her but she was stuck in the camp, patiently waiting her turn.

A heavy-set woman in her early thirties, Mrs. Guttman seemed to get heavier by the day even as everybody around her was losing weight because of the poor quality of food. Then, one day, the mystery was solved when Mrs. Guttman gave birth to a healthy baby girl and admitted she had been raped on the train by a Soviet soldier. Unfortunately, she had seizures quite often and we worried about the very real possibility that she might drop the baby. When we left the camp, she was still around. Perhaps the selecting committee was not eager to send her to a country already filled with problems.

Despite our new freedom and returning strength, Béla was gripped by depression caused by painful memories of his first wife and two sons who had been murdered. Although he preferred to stay home, he encouraged me to take advantage of the free time on our hands while we waited for our turn to leave. With his permission, I went on a number of excursions with friends to see the remarkable Italian countryside. It took a long time for us to be able to really enjoy the feeling that we were free and human again.

In the summer, we explored the northern region, the mountain area, and hitchhiked and attained free rides courtesy of the Italian railway system. Lake Como was our favourite destination. In Rome, we explored the Vatican, the Sistine Chapel with its indescribable wealth of sculptures, paintings, rare books and Michelangelo masterpieces. I was mesmerized by the statues of the Prophet Moses and King David. There was so much to see. We took in the old palaces, the Roman Colosseum, even the new parts of the city, with awe.

Another trip took us to Milan to explore and enjoy the dome with the golden roof. The hustle and bustle of the city was quite a contrast from the drab countryside we had left behind. We had money only for the cheapest tickets but we went to the opera and enjoyed the music all the same. With a loaf of bread and a tin of condensed milk, we fed ourselves and were happy. An occasional hot chocolate was the reward after a whole day's sightseeing when we retired to our cheap but clean hotel room.

We visited Venice and marvelled at the human ingenuity of how a city had been built on water. The architecture was remarkable. The Leaning Tower of Pisa was another adventurous excursion. We spent a week in Selvino, high up in the mountains, visiting a relative who was the supervisor of a home for Jewish orphans. The Italian government generously offered us lodging in a building that had been a luxurious summer home for those in the high echelons of the former fascist government.

Béla did join me for an excursion to a village where we rented a room from an old woman who lived alone with her goats and chickens. In the early morning, we watched the sunrise as the mist rose from the top of the mountains. It was a magnificent sight and made us feel happy to be alive. Walking down to the nearest village to catch the train back to town, we stopped by the fast-running creek to cool our feet. We enjoyed the gorgeous scenery, the fresh air and the echoing songs of the farmers who sang as they worked on the side of the mountain.

All this travelling came to an end after two years when my baby, Robert Eli, was born. I even gave up my teaching job to take care of my wonderful miracle. I had a difficult delivery because the hardships from the concentration camps had sapped my energy and made it harder for me to recuperate. Luckily, he was a happy, contented baby and gave us all the compensation we needed for the lost time and misery.

Robert Eli was just two months old when the independent Jewish state of Israel was declared. I will never forget the night the announcement came. Exulting in the good news, the whole camp was out singing and dancing by the torchlight in the huge garden. Barrels of beer were brought in, and our people were laughing and kissing each other as we prayed for a new era to begin.

By morning, the high spirit we felt the night before had been dampened by news that the Arab nations were preparing for war. We fell into a deep depression, anxious about the new state and its long-suffering people. We understood the seriousness of the situation, and as soon as the border was opened many young single men and women left the camp and went straight into army training. But our time hadn't come yet. We realized it would be too dangerous to take our tiny baby to Israel and decided to wait a little bit longer until the situation improved and peace arrived.

As we pondered our fate, a delegation from a Canadian trade union arrived looking for furriers. Without any serious questioning, they chose my husband, his brother and two nephews and their families. That is how we were included as part of a group of 150 families chosen to be some of the earliest immigrants to Canada after the war. Sick and tired of living in limbo, we chose Canada instead of Israel.

We had waited in the DP camp almost three years for a visa and were thrilled when it finally arrived. With great hopes, we were looking forward to our new life in this faraway land.

With our departure from Italy, we closed that chapter of our lives forever. Decades later, I returned with my son and daughter-in-law to see the town and hospital where my son was born. The visit brought back many bittersweet memories.

# Building a New Life

## IMMIGRATION TO CANADA

We boarded the MS *Sobieski*, the ship that would take us to Canada, at Genoa. The vessel, an old dilapidated ship that had been active throughout World War II, had originally belonged to Poland and was named after one of their kings. Our accommodations were far from luxurious. Refugees were assigned to the bottom of the ship: men in the front, women and children in the back, jammed together in an airless dark dormitory. The crossing was a nightmare. September is a bad month for sailing, especially on the bottom of a ship with crying babies and hysterical mothers arguing for space and a little privacy. The babies had quite comfortable hanging baskets but suffered from lack of nourishment. Since most of the nursing mothers couldn't eat because they were so seasick, they had no milk to feed the little ones. The adjoining part of the ship carried a cargo of iron rods and the long, narrow sticks rolled from side to side as the ship moved, making a horrible noise that made it difficult for us to sleep.

The first day, we were served a good meal on deck that everybody enjoyed. The waiters were kind and helpful, knowing very well that most of us would be seasick by the next day. As time went by, fewer and fewer passengers showed up each morning for breakfast. Lying on their cots, groaning with pain, they were unable to eat.

My baby, who had never had any solid food, just mother's milk, cried all the time and refused to take the bottle provided by the kitchen. My husband was also very sick. I got him baby food but he was unable to swallow it.

On the fourth day in this awful state, a kind stewardess summoned me to her cabin. On the table was a large plate of Italian noodles and a large glass of wine. She made me sit down and then ordered me in a strong authoritative voice to start eating. Just looking at the food made me sick and I protested that I couldn't swallow. But she wouldn't listen to my weak argument and warned me that if I wanted to see the other side of the ocean I had better start eating or both my baby and I would starve to death. She scared me so much that I pushed a forkful into my mouth. She made me drink a sip of wine and, slowly, I finished the meal, but I was barely able to keep it in my stomach.

"Now you can go," she ordered, "and make sure you do not miss any more meals." I never saw her again but I certainly felt much better after that. I was convinced that she was my guardian angel, sent from heaven to save my baby and me.

After the rough crossing on the high seas, we reached Halifax on September 19, 1948. Béla and I and our five-month-old son were some of the first displaced persons to be admitted to Canada after the war. After a long and tedious journey on a crowded train from Halifax, we arrived in Montreal. Rainy, grey weather welcomed us, along with a crew of indifferent personnel who could not communicate with the tired, irritated masses in their various languages. Eventually, we were taken to a government hotel outside Montreal where we were housed for a few days. We were interviewed there and officially processed with the necessary papers.

Béla, or Bill as he was called in Canada, had a contract with the government to work as a furrier and a job was guaranteed for him. But our limited knowledge of English made it quite difficult for us to understand what the officer was telling us. We eventually came to understand that we had the option to choose among Montreal, Winnipeg or Toronto. Our very limited knowledge of Canada made the discussion even harder. From school studies I remembered Ottawa as the capital city, and the "Indians" and "Eskimos" were familiar subjects to me. But neither of us had ever heard of the city of Toronto. Bill, being a practical man, considered the possibilities. Finding out that Montreal was bilingual, he ruled it out saying, "It is hard enough to learn one language at a time." He also ruled out Winnipeg because of its harsh cold winters. That's how we chose Toronto.

A few days later, we were on the train again, this time bound for Toronto. A welcoming committee from the Jewish community met us at the station and took us to a restaurant for our first real Canadian breakfast. We were very hungry and wolfed down the fresh bread and butter as if we had never eaten before.

A nice man from the committee took us to the flat that the Canadian Jewish Congress had assigned to us. It was almost impossible to find an apartment at that time, especially for a family with children. At first glance, the apartment left a lot to be desired. My first reaction was that I simply could not live in such a dirty place. However, I kept this to myself. I put my baby on top of our only suitcase, borrowed a pail from a neighbour and started to scrub down the walls and floor with a diaper. There was no running water in our flat, and so I had to carry water from the bathroom we shared with the other tenants. But, by evening, we were the proud owners of a bed and a blanket and a crib for the baby. There was a stove and icebox in the kitchen and orange crates to be used as a table and chairs. It was home. Bill went out shopping and returned with milk and bread. The next day, I cooked our first meal in Canada. We were content and eager to learn the customs of the land.

Bill started to work a few days later, and I was left on my own. It was hard to communicate with our neighbours without knowing English, but I had learned Yiddish, which was more useful than English for working in the garment industry. Everything was strange and difficult in the first few months. To make matters worse, our baby was infected with whooping cough, which he had contracted on the ship from the other children, so I was housebound with him for quite a while.

The house in which we lived was a microcosm of humanity — a miniature United Nations. The first floor was occupied by a friendly Polish couple with two small children, and the front room was rented out to Chinese girls who worked during the day. In the front room on the second floor lived Frau Rochele, an old woman who was one of only two survivors in her family. This poor woman worked as a seamstress all day and cried all night in her sleep for her nine murdered children and her husband. She loved our baby and kept an eye on my sleeping child while I did my shopping. The room and kitchen next door to us belonged to a couple with a child, also survivors of the Nazi labour camps. The top floor belonged to an Italian mother with a few noisy teenagers. Their kitchen was right above our bedroom, and, being a night person, she started her washing machine after midnight. As a result, we rarely had a night of uninterrupted sleep, which we needed so badly, and my baby had nightmares from the constant noise. But we suffered silently.

During our first year in Canada, our inadequate accommodations and taking care of a tiny infant in harsh conditions was very difficult. One washroom, used by all the tenants, served the entire house and we only had hot water for Christmas. We used the public steam bath on Spadina Avenue to take baths. Washing clothes was a big chore too. The water was carried in from the washroom and heated on the stove. The laundry was washed by hand and hung out on the radiators overnight to dry. One very hot summer night, our icebox overflowed and the water dropped down to the bedroom below. The neighbours complained to us that their bed was swimming in a pool of water. We could not do much, except apologize.

But as the old saying goes, "Where there's a will, there's a way." In the spring and summer, I loved the old tree-lined street where my baby learned to walk on the sidewalk and friendly neighbours stopped me to inquire about our well-being. I almost felt guilty to leave them after a year when we found a more decent place to bring up a child.

Although my husband's job as a furrier was secured by a government contract, the pay was low, but we were content that at least it covered the rent and put food on the table. I was anxious to start working too, if I could find a secure and loving environment for my little boy during the day. Daycare for the little ones was non-existent. Luckily, my niece, who arrived in Canada at the same time we did, offered to take care of Robert Eli since she was staying at home, expecting her first child. The arrangement worked out fine.

I got a job in a factory making bridal gowns, sewing buttons by the hundreds on the backs and sleeves of the pretty garments. The work hours were long, tiring and very boring. Occasionally, I looked out through the high window facing Lake Ontario and watched the shimmering water longingly. I felt trapped in the narrow workshop where I was doing the same tedious job day in and day out.

One day, one of the operators accidentally dropped one of the white garments on the floor and made it dirty. All the workers were swept up in a wave of panic. If the spot couldn't be cleaned, the poor woman would have to pay for the damage out of her own pocket. As the forewoman tried to clean the garment, we workers watched anxiously. My hands were still automatically sewing the buttons as my eyes concentrated on the cleaning process. Suddenly, Mr. Siegal, the owner, stopped by my table and sternly upbraided me in a loud voice. "In this country, everybody has to work," he said. "I don't pay for workers who are wasting time by taking it easy."

It took me a few seconds to understand that the sermon was addressed at me. My face turned red, my hands shook and my tears started to flow. Too shocked to respond to his accusations, I lost my voice. I got up from the work table, took my purse, walked over to the foreman and told him I was quitting. Then I walked toward the door. The incident created a commotion and the owner ran after me, asking me to stay. But I was so hurt I just turned around and left, crying all the way home.

I have to confess that my hard-working husband and his partners were more resilient than I was. When I dropped in at their workshop on the way home and told them the terrible way I had been treated, instead of sympathy they told me not to be so sensitive and not to take everything so seriously. But I was adamant that I wasn't going back to that factory. I started working at home, in our one-room apartment, as a dressmaker. Although we had no friends or relatives who could advise us, business soon began to arrive. Slowly, I built up a nice group of customers and supplemented my husband's small income. The bonus was that I had my baby with me, whose company I enjoyed, and nobody insulted me anymore.

The first piece of furniture we bought was my sewing machine. Our second possession was a little radio that became my steady companion. I listened to all types of lectures, debates, quiz shows, even kindergarten programming. Slowly, what I heard started to make sense to me as my ear got used to the steady flow of English. When my baby was old enough to go to nursery school, he became my real teacher, since he spoke perfect English in a short time. Five years later, my second child, Rochelle, came along. I spoke only English to her and, surprisingly, both my children grew up without any trace of my accent.

Since we had experienced some large-city life in Europe, we found the commuting easy in Toronto. But communication was another matter. Our favourite place to meet other newcomers was Queen's Park. We were drawn there magnetically in the hope of meeting someone from our former life. On weekends, we also liked to walk on College Street, where we met many newcomers with the same problems we had. The new friendships we forged helped compensate for the lack of our own families. Little by little, we got used to the new surroundings and the way of life that was very different from what we had left behind in Europe. We worked hard to make a living and, eventually, we made it. But accepting my losses and healing from the trauma of the war took a long time. We got to know and love this great city where we found our livelihood and our peace of mind.

For years afterwards, I kept in touch with a few of the ladies from the old street. I used to visit them with the children, whom they all generously loved and wanted to adopt. Now the street is there in name only, the people and the old houses are all gone. Only the memories remain.

## THE PEARL NECKLACE

I never stopped thinking about my parents and family who had been lost in the war. After many years of living in Canada, I found a pearl necklace in an antique store similar to the special pearl necklace my grandmother had worn before the war. When I noticed it, I started to cry because the pearls brought back many memories to me. I decided that I had to have those pearls at any price. My husband was generous and he bought them for me. The pearl necklace became a symbol to me of my former life and it completed a circle that was broken by our tragedy when I lost not only my family but also our personal possessions and the things that were dear to me. As I got older, I felt very strongly that my precious pearl necklace should go to my daughter who I felt was the rightful next link of the family heritage. She was very happy to receive it and wears it proudly.

## MY CAMP SISTER

At the Toronto Jewish Book Fair one year, I picked up a book that had been published in Italian and translated into English. The book was *Smoke Over Birkenau*, written by Liana Millu, an Italian Jew. When I started to read the book, a strange feeling came over me. I felt as if I could have written it. Here, again, was one more connection to the past. The story she told about her experiences in the Auschwitz-Birkenau death camp was my story too. She even wrote about how we celebrated Chanukah despite the danger of being caught by the Nazis. I realized that Liana and I had worked on the same road-building crew while in Auschwitz-Birkenau. Because we lived in the same barracks there, even her tattoo number was very close to mine. Like me, she had been shipped out to Germany via Ravensbrück and ended up in the large munitions factory in Malchow. We were also both liberated by the American army at the same time.

The whole book was a revelation and I felt I had to find this "lager sister," a camp sister, with whom I had so much in common. I didn't remember her face — fifty years is a long time — but I felt as if I had found a long-lost relative. I called the Italian Consulate in Toronto explaining my story and within half an hour I had Liana's address in Genoa. I wrote to her immediately, explaining my discovery and inviting her to visit me. Two weeks later, I received her answer. It was a happy day for me when I heard from her. She wrote:

*Dear Judith:*

*I was so deeply moved reading your letter. I have read it again and again. Certainly we were together in Birkenau, Ravensbrück and Malchow. This gives me a strange and beautiful feeling. Thank you for coming back into my life. After the war, I lived in Genoa again, my city. I was alone. I had nothing. It was a horrible period as I was trying to return to normal life again.*

*But I worked as a teacher and a writer. I am an old woman now but am still active in social programs. I feel it is my duty to deliver the message to young souls, to warn them about violence and its consequences. The memory of our inhuman treatment is still very much in my mind. We are the last eyewitnesses. Time is running out for our generation.*

*My life is full now, although I live alone. I have good friends, I have made peace with myself and I am satisfied. I always wished to visit*

*Canada but I am too old for travelling. I can travel in my dreams only.*
*Write to me, dear Judith. I will be grateful to hear from you again.*

*With love,*
*Liana Millu*
*Tattoo No. A.538p4*
*Buon Anno 1994*

It was exciting to have found Liana, a camp sister. Since Liana no longer travelled, I hoped to visit her with my son. Eli planned this trip, as he wanted to see the place where we had lived in the Displaced Persons camp in Turin, Italy, after the war. In April 1994, I travelled with Eli and his wife, Renée, from Turin to Genoa in order to meet Liana, retracing the route we had taken so many years before when, in 1948, we travelled from the DP camp to embark on our journey to Canada.

SÁRI

After the war I learned what had happened to my best friend, Sári, who had married so young back in Szerencs. When the Nazis occupied Hungary, Sári had been taken to a concentration camp with her entire family. Only the four sisters returned after the war, and Sári took over the responsibility of caring for them after her parents had been killed. A few months after liberation, she found out through the Red Cross that her husband was alive and on his way home. Shortly after his return, Sári and her husband emigrated to the United States where he had family. The former dentist became a farmer working hard just to earn his daily bread.

Sári was not content to only be a farmer's wife. She went back to school, took her studies very seriously and earned a diploma as a librarian. She raised two daughters and enjoyed her work. Over the years, we met many times and always enjoyed our reunions.

AUNTIE ROSIE

I often thought about the wonderful summers I had spent at my grandparents' homes, especially the attention and firm-but-loving discipline my maternal grandmother, Feige Leah Hofstadter, gave me. She was a very special woman who helped me through the trials and tribulations of growing up. Her approval of any decision I made was very important to me.

When my own children were growing up, they missed out on the love and emotional support only grandparents can give. Unfortunately, the entire older generation of our family was wiped out in the Shoah, so our whole family consisted only of young adults. While our children were very young, they didn't really know what they were missing, although I did. It was more difficult for me to raise them without the support and loving care of grandparents.

The real problems started when the children entered the school system. They realized the other children had something they had never experienced — grandparents. They had Bubbies and Zaides whom they visited or who came to visit them and with whom they exchanged gifts. All this made our children aware that they were missing an important part of the family structure. They often came home from school complaining. They wanted to know why other children had grandparents and they didn't. It was very difficult for me to explain since they were still too young to understand the tragedy that shadowed our lives.

Then a miracle happened. When the Hungarian Revolution started in 1956, the borders opened for a short while and freedom-loving people left the country. Many of them arrived in Toronto. They were a mass of tired, frustrated people without money or knowledge of the English language and little support from family or friends. The Canadian government did its best to accommodate them, but it was extremely difficult to absorb so many immigrants in such a short time. While they were looking for job opportunities and places to live, many of these new immigrants were sheltered temporarily at the Red Cross building, where they received the basic necessities.

Since I had been a newcomer fairly recently, I understood their multitude of problems and started to visit them regularly, offering assistance with language, housing and school registration for their children. I would also be there to just listen to their problems and complaints. I tried my best to help, but most of the issues were too big for me to resolve.

The most important part of my role, and that of other former Hungarians, was the encouragement we tried to give. We were sympathetic to the plight of these newcomers and told them that all their hardships would pass in good time.

On my very first visit to the centre, I met an older couple who were frightened and lonely and I felt as if I had known them for a long time. The woman was a very intelligent, sensitive person with a good sense of humour. The husband was just the opposite. He was already regretting that he had left the security and familiarity of his former home and worried terribly about how he would make a living without an applicable trade or any knowledge of English.

Rose Feigelstock was born in Hungary in 1908 and had worked as a dressmaker for many years. After her father retired, she became the sole supporter of her parents and younger siblings. She never complained and saw only the good side of people. She had average looks but her inner beauty shone through and her friendly smile and willingness to help the needy made her loved by her many friends. In Hungary, she had been more to her customers than just a dressmaker; she became their confidante and confessor. She advised them on what to buy, what styles were flattering and what to wear on special occasions.

The war ended that life, and Rose and her two younger sisters were the only survivors in their family. After liberation, they returned to the empty nest in a despondent, war-torn Hungary where opportunities to make a living were few. Eventually all three sisters married. Rose married a good-hearted man who promised to take care of her, but under the new communist-oriented regime their lot didn't improve much. During the 1956 uprising against the tyrannical government, they fled to Austria and then to Canada with the help of the Red Cross. That's when we first crossed paths.

Being bilingual in German and Hungarian, Rose quickly picked up Yiddish, an important asset in finding work in the garment trade in Toronto at that time. Her husband found a menial job in a bottle-washing plant, since his experience as a farmer was not much use in the city. With our help, Rose and her husband found a furnished apartment and slowly adjusted to the Canadian way of life. To ease their misery, I invited them to our house often, and they became part of our weekends and holidays. The children fell in love with the friendly couple instantly. Auntie Rosie, as they called her, showered them with hugs and kisses even when she wasn't able to talk to them in English.

Our son, Eli, was eight, and Rochelle was three at the time and they felt the love being lavished on them and gave the couple all their attention in return. One day, my daughter came up with a great idea. "Mommy," she said, "I want Auntie Rosie to be my grandmother."

At first I was stunned by the strange request. Then I realized what a wonderful solution this would be to fill the gap created by their missing grandparents. By that time, Auntie Rosie had a reasonable command of English, and Rochelle's Hungarian had improved. The very next opportunity she had, she shyly approached Auntie Rosie with her question. "Auntie Rosie, would you like to be my grandma, please?"

I watched the surprise and pleasure on Auntie Rosie's face. With a big smile, Auntie Rosie picked up the child and replied, with tears in her eyes, "Yes, darling, it will be an honour to be your grandma."

And so we acquired a grandma whose caring was genuine and sincere. After Rose's husband passed away, the bond she had with our family became even stronger. When my children had families of their own, we continued to include Rose as a member of the family at get-togethers, and my children would bring their children to visit Auntie Rosie when she moved to a senior citizens' home. Like any grandmother, she carried pictures of her grandchildren with her at all times, and when they came to visit she proudly presented them to her friends.

Being good-natured, Rose became everybody's friend in the senior citizens' home. For years she worked as a volunteer in the library and was very happy in her new home and environment. Unfortunately, her heart became very weak and she was transferred to the hospital for the aged. My family visited her regularly, and the bowls of fresh chicken soup or home-baked goods we brought her made her feel wanted and loved.

On my last visit with Rose, shortly before her ninetieth birthday, I had a premonition that it would be the last time I would see her. We had a very emotional talk about her forthcoming birthday and about my grandchildren, whom she loved dearly and called her sunshine kids. Unfortunately, a few days before her birthday, she fell and broke her hip. She ended up in the hospital, and after a painful operation her weak heart stopped working. She died three days before her ninetieth birthday.

Rose Feigelstock, our dear Rozsi Néni, touched the lives of many people, and we miss her and cherish her memory always.

MY FATHER'S DREAM

In 1992, my husband and I arrived in Israel in the middle of a rainstorm. Our family there was almost apologetic for the inconvenience the rain created and assured us they hadn't had weather like that for forty years. It dampened our spirits a bit to sit in the hotel room when we had such a great plan to spend our vacation outside. But the next day, the sun was shining again and people were swarming the promenade, enjoying the sea, the sun and the fresh air. As we sat on the chairs provided by the municipality and looked out at the ever-changing scenery of the sea, I had an eerie feeling of being in another

time and place. I could almost touch and see the face of my dear father, who had been killed by the Nazis almost fifty years earlier.

I remembered a woman whom I had known in Hungary and who
then moved from Montreal to Toronto after the war. This woman
told me she had encountered my father in Auschwitz. The revelation
shocked me because I hadn't realized my father had spent much time
there. I had heard he had been sent to work in a copper mine in Sile-
sia and had died there.

When she was in Auschwitz, this woman and my aunt, my mother's younger sister, were good friends. The woman had a six-year-old
child and my aunt had a sixteen-year-old daughter. Neither woman
knew what had happened to their children, and one day they decided
to smuggle themselves into the bathhouse in Auschwitz to see if anybody could give them some information about their children.

Naturally, they had to strip when they entered the bathhouse and,
all of a sudden, the door opened and my father walked in wearing a
striped uniform. My aunt recognized him right away and started to
cry as she tried to cover herself up.

"Don't cry," my father said, "and don't be ashamed. I don't see you
as you are now. I see you as I knew you before." Then he asked her
what they were doing in the bathhouse.

"We came to look for our children," my aunt replied.

"Try to get out of here as quickly as you can," my father told her,
"before they catch you. And don't you dare come here again. Don't
look for the children. Just make sure you get into a transport and
get out of Auschwitz as fast as you can. Whoever is here hasn't got a
chance. If you see my daughter, tell her that she should try to get out
of Auschwitz too. I'm hoping that I can get into a transport and out
of here because I have seen more than a person is supposed to see in
a lifetime."

And that was it. Soon after that, they shipped him out and she
never heard anything about him again.

As I sat by the sea in Israel, his smiling face was before me, so angelic, looking silently as I spoke to him. "Father" I said, "I never forgot how you taught us the love for the land which was only a dream to you. I am grateful for the legacy you left me. Now I have the responsibility to instill it in my children.

"I remember how you used to tell me about your dreams and hopes and that eventually we would all live together on this blood-and-tear-soaked land called Eretz Yisrael that was so far away from our home. You never gave up hope, even in the most dreadful days of our desperation. As the last straw of a drowning man, you registered your children to the Zionist organization, knowing full well that a great tragedy had come upon us and that we might be too late to fulfill your dream of settling in freedom and peace among our people in our own land.

"The dream shattered; you never had the zchus, merit, of seeing the miracle of the rebirth of Israel with your own eyes. But, Father, I am proud and grateful to tell you your struggle was not in vain. As much as I wanted to, I couldn't settle and live here in Israel. But I made sure your teaching was not forgotten. It was passed on to your grandchildren and will be passed on to the next generation.

"I am proud and grateful to be able to tell you that your namesake, your grandson, is helping to build the land. He is providing the much-needed work for new immigrants. He is a committed Jew, a real Zionist following in your footsteps. My dream is that what we missed, our grandchildren will continue. The broken chain will be mended and they will be the proud citizens in our land."

Seven years later, one morning in October 1999, my husband and I were having breakfast when the phone rang.

"Hello, Grandma, it's Tamar," a familiar voice said. "Mazel Tov, we have a girl and a boy."

I was stunned. "What did you say?" I yelled into the phone.

"A girl and a boy," she repeated.

"Let me sit down and tell me again," I answered.

"Grandma, it is a girl and a boy," she repeated again. "Here is Jono if you don't believe me. I am just out from the delivery room. Everything is fine."

"Mazel Tov. It's true, we have two babies," another excited voice came through the phone. "Do you hear me? Grandma, are you there?"

I was choking up with emotion and couldn't open my mouth, the tears running down my face. This was certainly a surprise. I knew my granddaughter and her husband who lived in Israel were expecting a baby and, whenever I had asked how she was feeling, the reply was always that everything was fine and going smoothly. But not a word was mentioned about twins. It took me a while to comprehend the great news, to realize how blessed we were to have had two healthy babies at the same time. We hope and pray they grow up to be healthy and happy beings, the pride and joy of our family.

FULL CIRCLE

One day in March 2005, a big envelope arrived in the mail for me from an unknown sender. Inside, to my great surprise, was a cheque for $1,000 and a very polite letter from a European insurance company. Evidently, after a long search through their archives, this insurance company found the evidence of my right to the insurance money my father had diligently put away for me all those years ago. I had married, settled in Canada and raised two beautiful children who grew up to have families of their own. The insurance policy that Yitzhak had ripped up out of anger in Hungary after the war had made its way to Canada.

Reading that letter brought my whole past back to life again for me. The insurance company's letter arrived almost exactly sixty years after the evil nightmare that the Nazis had inflicted upon the Jews of Hungary. In memory of my father, I sent the money to my poor relatives in Israel. I am sure that his soul would be pleased.

# Rediscovering Family and Unexpected Reunions

MY COUSIN ILUS

I only learned what happened to Ilus, my cousin whom I had looked up to when I was so much younger in Hungary, many years later. Ilus and her husband, Dezső, had been married ten years when World War II broke out. Her parents and siblings had left together for America years earlier. When the war started, Dezső was called into the Hungarian army and later sent to the labour camps when Jews were expelled from regular army service. He was assigned to a unit to clear mines, a dangerous and usually fatal service. A short time later, Ilus was advised by the Red Cross that her husband was missing in action. This usually meant that the man had been killed somewhere on the Soviet front.

Ilus mourned her husband and missed him terribly, but life went on. Her husband's partner carried on their business and shared the profit he made equally with her so she had no financial problems. When the Nazis occupied Hungary, the real trouble started for Jewish people in Hungary and for Ilus. Jews were moved into ghettos, a condition of unbearable misery. Since Ilus was alone, with no family to take care of, it was easier for her to escape from this hell on earth. With her good looks and the help of false identification papers, Ilus slipped out of the ghetto and made her way to the capital city, Budapest, where it was easier to hide her real identity. She found a job as a waitress in a bar and worked there until the Soviet army liberated the city. By that time, some of her extended family had been deported and killed in Auschwitz. Luckily, her parents, two brothers and two sisters had managed to escape just in time to the United States.

When she was finally liberated, there was hunger and misery all around her. The Soviets picked people up indiscriminately on the streets and, without asking questions, shipped them to the Soviet Union for forced labour. Returning to her hometown, Ilus was looking for food when two soldiers threw her in with other stragglers who were then all taken to a gathering station to await deportation. After liberation from a concentration camp, her husband's former partner, Sandor, had made his way home too. His family had been wiped out and he was in great despair. When he found out about Ilus's escape from the ghetto, he started to look for her. After a long search, he traced her to the detention camp and managed to snatch her out of the column that was getting ready to leave Hungary.

The once-beautiful Ilus was in a terrible mental and physical state. Almost a skeleton, full of lice, her old clothes in tatters, she gratefully took Sandor's helping hand. He found her a place to live and got her food and clothing as she slowly regained her health and self-esteem. She waited patiently, praying and hoping that a miracle would return her husband to her.

While she kept herself busy, trying to live a normal life by cooking and doing chores, Sandor re-established the business they had before the war, slowly getting back to a normal existence and again sharing the profit he made with her.

A few years passed and still there was no word of the missing husband. Then, one day, a good friend of the family was released from a Soviet labour camp and returned to Hungary. He visited Ilus and told her the sad news that he had been with her husband for a long time when they worked in the same battalion. One day, both had ended up in the hospital seriously ill. A few nights later, the orderlies took her husband out of the ward. It was common practice to dispose of dead bodies in the middle of the night and, naturally, he assumed that Dezső was dead. When the friend tried to find out his fate, nobody seemed to know what had happened to him.

Ilus was very sad when she received the bad news, but life went on. Since Sandor was lonely too, they saw each other often. Ilus would invite him over for home-cooked meals and he was very grateful for the attention he received from her. Slowly, he fell in love with her. A while later, they decided to get married and try to make the best of their lives, which now had a new meaning. He became a loving husband, and she blossomed as they tried to put the past behind them and have a happy life together.

When Ilus and Sandor had been married for about a year, Ilus's first husband, Dezső, suddenly walked back into their lives. He had been released from the camp and claimed his right to his wife. She was in a terrible dilemma as to what to do. She had to first divorce both husbands. Feeling great pressure from both of them, Ilus then decided to stay with the second husband, whom she had learned to love and respect. They got married again and carried on with their lives as best they could. But the shadow of the first husband hung over them and made her feel uneasy. Dezső didn't remarry and still only loved Ilus. Then tragedy struck again. Sandor developed a brain tumour and died after a short and painful illness, leaving Ilus in a state of shock.

By then, the political situation had also changed in Hungary. The Communist regime did not tolerate private enterprises, so the good business, the carefree life, was gone. Ilus, for the first time in her life, had to go to work to keep herself alive. Since she had no training in any field to make a living, she was struggling to provide the bare necessities for herself. Dezső again appeared on the scene and asked her to marry him. After much soul-searching, she consented. She was a good wife to him and he was a good provider, but the spark of their former life was gone forever.

A few years later, during the Hungarian Uprising of 1956, the borders were opened for a few days, and Ilus and her husband decided to leave Hungary to establish a new life in a new country. They emigrated to the United States, where her parents, my Uncle Herman and Aunt Czili, brothers and sisters helped them get settled. Her husband spoke no English but found a job doing manual labour, and she became the nursemaid for her ailing, elderly parents. The beautiful carefree life she had lived before the war was long gone. She became a drab housewife with a lot of feelings of guilt.

We had been living in Canada for a few years when they immigrated to America. When we were reunited, I was still very much attached to my beautiful cousin and tried to find the Ilus of old. I invited them often to our house and they loved our children who filled the void a little in their empty lives.

In her later life, when both of her parents were dead, Ilus had lots of time to think and she became paranoid, gained weight and hated herself for it. She complained all the time. The past haunted her to the point that she lived in imaginary terror. The doctors gave her drugs that made her listless, and she died a few years after her husband, a lonely miserable person for whom life had lost its meaning.

~

I also found out years after the war that Ilus's brothers, my cousin Nick, with whom I had been so close in my youth, and his elder brother, Ernő, had both fought in the American army, trying to liberate us from our deadly enemies. It was a few years after my husband and I and our son had settled in Canada that I was reunited with my cousin Nick again. It was always a joy to see him or talk to him on the phone. I also became close to Nick's wife, Erika, a fine person, and I felt as if I had known her always. Her gentle nature and quiet personality made her a great woman and a good mother and grandmother.

A JOURNEY OF REUNIONS

In 1966, Irene Goldschmidt, a good friend who lived in Buenos Aires, Argentina, invited us to her son's bar mitzvah. Since it was in the middle of a very cold winter in Toronto, Béla and I decided to accept their kind offer to enjoy a little sunshine while celebrating with our dear friends. This trip, which came to also include Uruguay and Rio de Janeiro, Brazil, turned out to be an important trip full of reunions.

Part of our journey to South America brought us to Rio de Janeiro for a few days. Not knowing anyone, we took a tour and enjoyed the sights of the world's most beautiful city. On the Sabbath, we visited a small synagogue by the ocean and met people who were very friendly, one of whom invited us for an afternoon tea. During our conversation, they wanted to know where we came from. We discovered that a good friend of theirs in Rio de Janeiro might be a granddaughter of my aunt Serel Hofstadter (Ehrenfeld).

Right after Shabbat had ended, our hostess made a phone call and quickly determined that the woman whom she had called was my second cousin Giselle Demajo.

My maternal grandfather, Aryeh Leib Hofstadter, had an older sister, Serel, who had lived in the town of Zenta, Yugoslavia. Serel had two daughters and a son, who were among the first victims of the aerial bombing by the Americans in World War II. The older daughter, Chana, had had three daughters and two sons. Since my family and the whole Hofstadter clan lived in Hungary and Chana's children still lived in Yugoslavia, the border restrictions meant that we had very little contact with them.

World War II and the Holocaust killed almost all these family members, and the few cousins who survived emigrated to various countries, so we never heard of them again. After becoming orphaned and ending up in Canada, I imagined I was one of the few who had survived.

But then here I was on the phone with my cousin Giselle. An excited conversation ensued as both of us asked questions at the same time. Then I heard her call to her husband in a high-pitched voice, "Stevo, I am not an orphan anymore! I found my family." It was too late in the evening to meet our new-found relatives, so we suggested an early morning meeting, explaining that we had to catch a flight to Venezuela at seven the following morning.

"You are not going anywhere until I see you," answered Giselle. "We are coming early and you make your plans afterwards, cancel the taxi and that's final." I couldn't sleep that night; I was so excited to see my newly discovered relatives.

Early in the morning, there was a rap on the door. When I opened it, there was a middle-aged woman with deep-set eyes like my late grandfather's looking at me. Crying and laughing, kissing and hugging, we confirmed the discovery that we were relatives, no question about it. We just couldn't get over the lucky coincidence.

Giselle and Stevo took us to the airport with the promise that they would come to visit us in Canada soon. That summer, they came to Toronto and met the rest of our family. When they told us their story we understood the miracle of their survival.

Giselle came from an Orthodox Jewish background. She was a very talented artist, and the town where she was raised was too small for her ambition. After a painful departure from her family, she moved to Belgrade, the capital of Yugoslavia. There she met Stevo, a highly educated, wonderful human being from a traditional Sephardic home. They fell in love and married.

Stevo had been a high-ranking officer in the Yugoslav army when the German military overran the country in 1941. The Germans' first action was to pluck all the Jewish soldiers out of the army and use them for dangerous jobs like picking up mines on the front lines. It was obvious that life was getting more difficult by the day under the Germans. War was already looming when the young couple wed, and by the time they tried to leave all the borders were closed — there was little hope of escape.

Giselle made contact with an old peasant who smuggled people over the border to Italy. When she located him, he was in the hospital after surgery and was very sick. He was in great pain and told Giselle he couldn't help her. Giselle, being good-hearted, felt sorry for him because the man had no family to take care of him. She went home and baked a cake with her last two eggs, which she then took to the sick man. He was so impressed with her thoughtfulness that he promised to help her. He made arrangements for somebody to smuggle Giselle and Stevo out of Yugoslavia. Stevo didn't want to go on such a dangerous journey, but Giselle was determined.

A Nazi sympathizer lived on the same floor as Giselle and Stevo in their apartment block and he put fear into most residents' hearts. Giselle boldly knocked on his door, introduced herself and told him their plan to escape, telling him that she put their lives at his mercy. The Nazi was obviously shocked by her honesty and gave them advice on how to get out of the building unnoticed. He told Giselle to tell Stevo to shave off his moustache and take a tranquilizer before leaving. Then he wished them luck.

The plan worked. They presented themselves as "Aryan" refugees and moved to Italy, which even under Mussolini's fascist regime was known to be more humane. Giselle and Stevo lived in a small village under constant surveillance by the police, but they felt their lives were not in danger. The villagers were good and tolerant people, but the war was taking its toll on their lives. Food was scarce and life was harsh for everyone. Slowly, though, the couple learned the language while they waited for the war to end.

One day, they heard that the Red Cross of Switzerland had picked up a planeload of little children from war-torn Yugoslavia whose parents had been killed or interned and planned to settle them temporarily in Italy until peace was restored. Unfortunately, the plane crashed and there were few survivors. The lucky ones were taken to the hospital with serious injuries.

My cousins decided that they wanted to take care of one of the children. They applied to the hospital and got permission to take a little girl who was in a very poor physical and emotional state. She was a lovely child with blond hair and beautiful blue eyes; it was an instant love affair between my cousins and their new ward. With great patience, they earned her trust and restored her health by sharing their meagre food supplies. A few years later, when the war was nearly over, my cousins' hope was restored and they planned to adopt their charge and officially claim her as their own. Even after Yugoslavia was liberated, however, people there were still not free to travel.

One day, a man was walking on the street with a little girl who was wearing a red, checkered coat. A young woman saw them from across the street, ran over and excitedly claimed the girl was her daughter. The woman was sure, she said, because she had made the red coat the child was wearing for her daughter before putting her child on the airplane to Italy.

The man got very agitated and started yelling that perhaps the coat was made by the woman but the child was his for sure. A large crowd gathered and listened to the argument until a policeman appeared. He listened to both parties' tales. After a heated argument, both parties decided to turn to the Red Cross to find out how this little girl came to be wearing the coat made by this woman.

Before long, the mystery was solved. The coat really belonged to the woman's little girl but the wearer of the coat was not hers. With the help of the Red Cross, they found the original owner of the coat, the young girl in the care of my cousins. With broken hearts, they had to return their beloved little girl to the real mother and father, who had miraculously escaped the Nazis. The girl and her real parents emigrated to Israel shortly thereafter.

Giselle and Stevo did eventually return from Italy to their hometown in Yugoslavia. They were shocked to find a ghost town — not one relative had survived. With broken hearts, they moved to Brazil. In Brazil, they tried to rebuild their lives, believing no one else in their family was alive.

They kept in touch with the girl they had loved and cared for in Italy, who blossomed in Israel into a beautiful young woman. She now lived in Nahariya and was married with grown children, but the love she had had for my cousins was still alive. Some years ago, a handsome young man knocked on Stevo and Giselle's door in Brazil. "My mother sent me to you," he said. "If you hadn't raised her, I would never have been born."

Now, with another rap at the door, Giselle and Stevo had welcomed more relatives, Béla and me, into their lives, and they were overwhelmed with the knowledge that they still had family who had survived. We forged a wonderful relationship. We loved them and spent many happy times together in our home and theirs. Our children benefited from their love and wisdom. Unfortunately, we lost both of them too soon, but their memory will live with us for as long as we are alive.

We also learned that the man who had helped arrange to smuggle Giselle and Stevo over the border had been pulled from his sickbed by the Nazis and hanged. He was a great man who should be remembered for having saved the lives of Jews. May his soul be blessed.

Maya Giselle, my great-granddaughter, was named after my dear cousin Giselle, so now we have another Giselle in the family.

~

Giselle was not the only family member with whom we were reunited on this trip to South America. By a fortuitous coincidence, we met Uncle Eugene Schwarcz's youngest son soon after our arrival. However, since he had been born in Argentina, he had very little knowledge of the Hungarian history of his family. After discovering who we were, he contacted his parents. We had a very emotional reunion. We were incredibly happy to re-establish contact with this family. The distinguished old couple with snow-white hair and rosy cheeks sat holding hands and listened to my story of the tragedy that had befallen us. They also shared their story with me and Béla. Eugene Schwarcz had been my father's best friend.

Eugene Schwarcz grew up in the same town as my father and went to school with him. My father and Eugene kept up a warm friendship even after our family moved to Szerencs. Uncle Eugene, as we called him even though we were not actually related, got married at the same time as my father and mother did and had a lovely wife and two sons. He owned a dry goods store and made a good living until the worldwide Great Depression hit Hungary. Uncle Eugene lost his livelihood — nothing was left of the comfortable living he had previously provided for his family.

Out of desperation, he turned to his old friend, my father, hoping he would be able to help him. Eugene had a brother in Argentina who was willing to send him the necessary papers, but he had no means to buy him the ticket. Father was not in a position to give him the necessary money, but he had a few well-to-do friends who were willing to help. The money was collected and a grateful Eugene sailed to Argentina with his oldest son, who was about ten years old. Two years later, Uncle Eugene was able to send tickets to his wife and younger son to join them. We heard from them occasionally and knew they had settled in Buenos Aires, where one more son was born to complete their family.

With Hitler rising to power in Germany, people in Europe were becoming increasingly worried, especially the Jews. The propaganda was so powerful that we didn't know what the real situation was. One day, my father received a letter from Uncle Eugene advising us to get serious about emigration. He wanted to return the favour my father had done for them and was willing to send us the necessary papers to settle in Argentina.

My father took the offer seriously. However, after discussing it with my grandparents and his brothers, he decided to stay, thinking, as many others did, that the Nazi scare would pass and everything would be back to normal soon. We paid for our false hopes greatly, since only a handful of the young ones survived from our once-large and extended family.

After hearing their story and recounting my sad tale to Uncle Eugene and his wife, I felt it was an appropriate time to warn them of the danger of living under a strong military regime. A few years after my husband and I settled in Canada, I read in the paper about the terrible situation existing under the military regime in Argentina. The witch hunt against communism seemed frightening, and I had often wondered whether Uncle Eugene's family was safe or whether they would become innocent victims of the junta rulers.

Uncle Eugene happily reported the good news that he was in the process of immigrating to Israel with their son and his family. Another son had already made the transition and had made sure that they would all be comfortable in their new homes. The following year, we visited them in Israel. Contented and happy to be among their own family, they lived out their lives in peace and were buried in the city of Petah Tikva, Israel, the city of hope.

~

This trip also made possible my reunion with Anci Tenenbaum. Anci and I became dear friends while we lived in the Displaced Persons camp in Italy. We had so much in common, having our babies at the same time and having suffered similar hardships during the war. Anci had great common sense and was easy to talk to. We thought alike and I loved her dearly. Life was difficult in the DP camp, and many problems arose which were impossible to solve. Everybody needed a good person with whom to share the ever-present dilemmas of how to carry on with life — Anci and I were there for each other.

When we received the permit to immigrate to Canada after three years in the camp, we had to say goodbye to our dear friends. With many tears, we promised that we would stay in touch no matter where our fate took us. It took twenty-five years of searching to find the Tenenbaums again. By sheer luck, a stranger who was visiting Toronto brought us the first news of them in all these years. The information was very brief, but we learned that they were well and living in Uruguay.

During our trip to Argentina, the weather was sunny at first but then turned cold and rainy. Bill began to get restless and was ready to move on. On a whim, we decided to look up Anci and her family in Montevideo, Uruguay. It took an hour to fly to Montevideo. As soon as we settled into our hotel room, I picked up the telephone book to try to find our friend's address and telephone number. I started to panic when I realized that they were not listed in the directory.

With a sinking heart, I tried to figure out how to find our friends in a strange city without knowing a soul or even speaking the local language. As I was thinking about a solution, I recalled an incident that had happened in the New York airport before we boarded the plane to our destination. A friendly middle-aged man had started to talk to us and wanted to know where we were going. He spoke Hungarian and told us that he lived in Uruguay and would be changing planes in Rio de Janeiro in order to get home. He asked if I could do him a favour and help carry an extra bag since he had too many parcels. I had only one handbag so I couldn't refuse him and took his bag to the airplane. He was very grateful for the favour and gave me his address. He told us that if we ever visited Montevideo, he would be honoured to have us as his guest.

I had put away his card, not paying much attention to it, but now was the moment to cash in on the favour I had done him. I called his number and spoke to him. He happened to know our friends and gave me their phone number!

My husband called the office where Anci's husband, Miklos Te-nenbaum, worked, and within a short time Miklos knocked on our door. There was great excitement when we met, with hugging and kissing. It was a very emotional meeting as we struggled to find the right words after so many years. Miklos picked up our suitcases and, despite our vehement protests, was determined to take us to his home as his personal guests. When we arrived at his apartment, Miklos called up to his wife on the building's intercom to tell her that he had brought guests. A few minutes later, Anci was standing in the doorway, looking at us. She rubbed her eyes and, with a loud cry, hugged and kissed us.

I will never forget that weekend. Twenty-five years of catching up in one weekend as we held hands and cried the whole time. We cried for and lamented the lost years, the years when we could have enjoyed each other's company. But fate had dealt with us otherwise. When we parted, we promised not to let history repeat itself and to stay in touch, no matter what.

Anci and Miklos, the ever-optimistic couple, decided to emigrate once more in their lifetime. They also settled down in Israel, where their daughter Vera had already made her home. Whenever I went to Israel, Anci, my dear adopted sister, welcomed me with open arms. We always had so much to catch up on. The feelings we had toward each other never changed, but our deep affection for each other just increased with the joy of being able to share about our extended families and the great pleasure our grandchildren gave us.

The last time I said goodbye to my adopted sister, my confidante and loving friend, I never thought it would be the last time we would be together. Even today I cry when I think of her loving kindness. Dearest friend, may God give peace to your *neshama*, your soul.

A CHANCE MEETING AT A CHARITY TEA

One day, a group of dedicated women decided to organize a charity tea party to take place during Chanukah, the Jewish Festival of Light. The woman in charge of the evening knew me and asked me to talk to the guests about the miracle of survival of my generation. I agreed to tell them my life story in a nutshell, the unbelievable experiences that happened to me and my friends while we were captive in Auschwitz.

While I was waiting for the program to begin, the woman who had invited me introduced me to a young woman named Angie, who I was told was a very special person because she had been born in Auschwitz.

I was excited to hear this unusual news and was anxious to find out how she had survived in the death camp — since over a million healthy Jewish children were killed by the Nazis during the Holocaust. If a baby was born in Auschwitz, the baby and the mother were murdered together. Looking at her with great curiosity, I asked her which part of Europe she came from.

"I lived in a town named Sárospatak, Hungary. That's where I grew up and went to school."

"One of my dear friends, who shared the wooden plank with me where we slept with ten other women, was from the same town," I told her. "We worked on the same road-building crew. I was shipped to Germany to work in a munitions factory and lost contact with her. After liberation, I searched for her but nobody had heard of her. I took it for granted that she was killed with the thousand other unfortunates. Her name was Vera Bein."

The young woman looked at me with unbelieving eyes. "You knew Vera Bein? She was my mother."

We looked at each other speechlessly and then, with a hug and a cry, were clinging to each other. Angie, once she had recovered from the shock, began to tell me her and her mother's story. Yes, she had been born in Auschwitz, a few days before Christmas 1944. Her mother, Vera, was very thin from the starvation diet and hard work and gave birth to a two-pound baby. The newborn was so weak she had no voice and couldn't even cry.

Immediately after having the baby, her mother bundled her in rags and put her up on the highest shelf to hide her from the Nazi inspections, hoping they wouldn't find out about her. Then she went out to stand in the early morning roll call. She would have only had water to drink because food was not available in the camp by then, so it was a miracle she had enough milk to nurse her baby. Soon after Angie's birth, the fighting on the Soviet front came close to Auschwitz and the Nazis were preparing for the evacuation of the camp.

Every able-bodied person was marched out on the road and the death march began. Vera concealed her baby under her coat and went on the march too. It was the middle of January and they were without food and warm clothes. Whoever was not able to move was shot by the guards immediately.

This brave mother tried to walk with thousands of others but her strength gave out, finally, and she couldn't move anymore. She sat down at the side of the road, ready to give up the struggle. Miraculously, the guards didn't notice her and she was left behind. She ate snow, nursed her baby and waited. A few days later, the camps were liberated by the Soviet army, and mother and baby were free at last. The Soviet soldiers were kind to the refugees, took care of their illnesses and fed them well. But instead of sending the refugees back to their original homes, the Soviets shipped them to the Soviet Union. It took almost a year before mother and baby could make their way back to their hometown.

Vera's husband never returned after the war, and Vera struggled to keep herself and her baby alive. Eventually, she remarried a kind man who adopted little Angie and raised her as his own. When her husband died of heart failure a few years later, Vera immigrated to Canada and settled in Toronto. By that time, Angie was married and followed her mother to Canada a few years later with her husband and little daughter.

Vera died a year before I met Angie. Unfortunately, I never had a chance to meet her again. It pains me to think of the lost opportunity for a happy reunion.

Holding Angie's hand, I told the listening ladies about this unusual chance meeting and assured them that, "yes, miracles can still happen."

# Glossary

*Appell* (German) Roll call.

*aron-koydesh* (Yiddish; Holy Ark) The place in a synagogue where the Torah scrolls are kept.

**Arrow Cross Party** (in Hungarian, Nyilaskeresztes Párt – Hungarista Mozgalom; abbreviation: Nyilas) A Hungarian nationalistic and antisemitic party founded by Ferenc Szálasi in 1935 under the name the Party of National Will. With the full support of Nazi Germany, the newly renamed Arrow Cross Party ran in Hungary's 1939 election and won 25 per cent of the vote. The party was banned shortly after the elections, but was legalized again in March 1944 when Germany occupied Hungary. Under Nazi approval, the party assumed control of Hungary from October 15, 1944, to March 1945, led by Szálasi under the name the Government of National Unity. The Arrow Cross regime was particularly brutal toward Jews — in addition to the thousands of Hungarian Jews who had been deported to Nazi death camps during the previous Miklós Horthy regime, the Arrow Cross, during their short period of rule, instigated the murder of tens of thousands of Hungarian Jews. In one specific incident on November 8, 1944, more than 70,000 Jews were rounded up and sent on a death march to Nazi camps in Austria. Between December 1944 and January 1945, the Arrow Cross murdered approximately 20,000 Jews, many of whom had been forced into a closed ghetto at the end of November 1944.

**Auschwitz** (German; in Polish, Oświęcim) A town in southern Poland approximately forty kilometres from Krakow, it is also the name of the largest complex of Nazi concentration camps that were built nearby. The Auschwitz complex contained three main camps: Auschwitz I, a slave labour camp built in May 1940; Auschwitz II-Birkenau, a death camp built in early 1942; and Auschwitz-Monowitz, a slave labour camp built in October 1942. In 1941, Auschwitz I was a testing site for usage of the lethal gas Zyklon B as a method of mass killing, which then went into wide usage. Between 1942 and 1944, transports arrived at Auschwitz-Birkenau from almost every country in Europe — hundreds of thousands from both Poland and Hungary, and thousands from France, the Netherlands, Greece, Slovakia, Bohemia and Moravia, Yugoslavia, Belgium, Italy and Norway. As well, more than 30,000 people were deported there from other concentration camps. It is estimated that 1.1 million people were murdered in Auschwitz; approximately 950,000 were Jewish; 74,000 Polish; 21,000 Roma; 15,000 Soviet prisoners of war; and 10,000–15,000 other nationalities. The Auschwitz complex was liberated by the Soviet army in January 1945.

**Auschwitz Uprising** (also known as the Sonderkommando Uprising) A coordinated attempt by *Sonderkommando* workers — the concentration camp prisoners ordered to remove corpses from the gas chambers, load them into the crematoria and dispose of the remains — to destroy the crematoria facilities at Auschwitz-Birkenau on October 7, 1944.

*beit hamidrash* (Hebrew; Yiddish, *beys midrash*; house of learning) A Jewish religious study centre.

**Bnei Akiva** (Hebrew; children of Akiva) The youth wing of the Orthodox Mizrachi Zionist movement founded in British Mandate Palestine in 1929 and still in existence internationally today. Their philosophy is that *Torah*, or religious commitment, and *Avodah*, work, go hand in hand. The concept of *Avodah* was initially interpreted as agricultural work but today has a broader definition of work that helps Israel develop as a modern state.

**British Mandate Palestine** The area of the Middle East under British rule from 1923 to 1948, as established by the League of Nations after World War I. During that time, the United Kingdom severely restricted Jewish immigration. The Mandate area encompassed present-day Israel, Jordan, the West Bank and the Gaza Strip.

**cantor** (in Hebrew, *chazzan*) A person who leads a Jewish congregation in prayer. Because music plays such a large role in Jewish religious services, the cantor is usually professionally trained in music.

**Chanukah** (also Hanukkah; Hebrew; dedication) An eight-day festival celebrated in December to mark the victory of the Jews against foreign conquerors who desecrated the Temple in Jerusalem in the second century BCE. Traditionally, each night of the festival is marked by lighting an eight-branch candelabrum called a menorah to commemorate the rededication of the Temple and the miracle of its lamp burning for eight days without oil.

**Eretz Yisrael** (Hebrew) The biblical Land of Israel.

*feldsher* (Russian) Medic or physician's assistant. Healthcare professional who provided many medical services in the Soviet Union, mainly in rural areas.

**ghetto** A confined residential area for Jews. The term originated in Venice, Italy, in 1516 with a law requiring all Jews to live on a segregated, gated island known as Ghetto Nuovo. Throughout the Middle Ages in Europe, Jews were often forcibly confined to gated Jewish neighbourhoods. During the Holocaust, the Nazis forced Jews to live in crowded and unsanitary conditions in rundown districts of cities and towns.

**Hungarian Uprising** (also Hungarian Revolution; 1956) A spontaneous uprising against the Soviet-backed Communist government of Hungary in October 1956, the Hungarian Revolution led to the brief establishment of a reformist government under Prime Minister Imre Nagy. The revolution was swiftly crushed by the Soviet invasion of November 1956, during which thousands of civilians were killed.

**Judenrat** (German; pl. *Judenräte*) Jewish Council. A group of Jewish leaders appointed by the Germans to administer and provide services to the local Jewish population under occupation and carry out Nazi orders. The *Judenräte*, which appeared to be self-governing entities but were actually under complete Nazi control, faced difficult and complex moral decisions under brutal conditions and remain a contentious subject. The chairmen had to decide whether to comply or refuse to comply with Nazi demands. Some were killed by the Nazis for refusing, while others committed suicide. Jewish officials who advocated compliance thought that cooperation might save at least some of the population. Some who denounced resistance efforts did so because they believed that armed resistance would bring death to the entire community.

**Kanada** A name given to the warehouses that stored the belongings and clothing confiscated from newly arrived prisoners in Auschwitz. The name, adopted by the prisoners working there, came from the widely held belief that Canada was a land of wealth, thus its association with the enormous amount of goods seized by the camp authorities. The workers given the task of sorting these items were referred to as the Kanada *Kommando*.

**Kommando** (German; literally, unit or command) Forced work details that were set up by the Nazi labour and concentration camp administrators during World War II.

**Malchow** An external subcamp of Ravensbrück concentration camp located at the German town of Malchow. Prisoners from Ravensbrück were first transported to Malchow to provide labour in the ammunition plant there in the winter of 1943–44. The camp's role as a labour camp declined with the extreme overcrowding

in February 1945, with many more inmates arriving from evacuated eastern camps. The concentration camp, including living
barracks, a wash barracks and an infirmary barracks, was on the
verge of collapse from the end of March 1945, with the remaining
women led out of the camp on a death march on May 1, 1945.

**matzah** (Hebrew; also matza, matzoh, matzot, matsah; in Yiddish,
matze) Crisp flatbread made of plain white flour and water that is
not allowed to rise before or during baking. Matzah is the substi-
tute for bread during the Jewish holiday of Passover, when eating
bread and leavened products is forbidden. *See also* Pesach.

*Megillah* The scroll of the Book of Esther, which is traditionally read
during the holiday of Purim. *See also* Purim.

**Mengele, Josef** (1911–1979) The most notorious of about thirty SS
garrison physicians in Auschwitz. Mengele was stationed at the
camp from May 1943 to January 1945; from May 1943 to August
1944, he was the medical officer of the Birkenau "Gypsy Camp";
from August 1944 until Auschwitz was evacuated in January 1945,
he became Chief Medical Officer of the main infirmary camp
in Birkenau. One of the camp doctors responsible for deciding
which prisoners were fit for slave labour and which were to be immediately sent to the gas chambers, Mengele was also known for
conducting sadistic experiments on Jewish and Roma prisoners,
especially twins.

*mishloach manot* (Hebrew; also *shalach-manos*, literally, sending of
portions) A gift basket sent on the holiday of Purim. The tradition
comes from the Book of Esther and is considered a mitzvah (a
good deed), as it involves providing people with food to celebrate
the holiday. *See also* Purim.

**Organization for Rehabilitation through Training (ORT)** A voca-
tional school system founded for Jews by Jews in Russia in 1880.
The name ORT derives from the acronym of the Russian organization Obshestvo Remeslenogo Zemledelcheskogo Truda, Society for Trades and Agricultural Labour.

**Pesach** (Hebrew; also Passover) One of the major festivals of the Jewish calendar, Pesach takes place over eight days in the spring. One of the main observances of the holiday is to recount the story of Exodus, the Jews' flight from slavery in Egypt, at a ritual meal called a seder. The name itself refers to the fact that God "passed over" the houses of the Jews when he set about slaying the first-born sons of Egypt as the last of the ten plagues aimed at convincing Pharaoh to free the Jews. *See also* seder.

**Purim** (Hebrew; literally, lots) The celebration of the Jews' escape from annihilation in Persia. The Purim story recounts how Haman, advisor to the King of Persia, planned to rid Persia of Jews, and how Queen Esther and her cousin Mordecai foiled Haman's plot by convincing the king to save the Jews. During the Purim festivities, people dress up as one of the figures in the Purim story, hold parades and retell the story of Haman, Esther and Mordecai.

**Ravensbrück** The largest Nazi concentration camp created almost exclusively for women that was established in May 1939 and located about ninety kilometres north of Berlin. Throughout the war, subcamps were built in the area around Ravensbrück to serve as forced labour camps. From 1942 on, the complex served as one of the main training facilities for female SS guards. Medical experiments were carried out on the women at Ravensbrück, and in early 1945 the SS built a gas chamber, where approximately 5,000 to 6,000 prisoners were murdered. More than 100,000 women prisoners from all over Nazi-occupied Europe had passed through Ravensbrück before the Soviets liberated the camp on April 29-30, 1945. Approximately 50,000 women died in the camp.

**seder** (Hebrew; literally, order) A ritual family meal celebrated at the beginning of the festival of Passover. *See also* Pesach.

*seuda* (Hebrew; literally, meal) The term is used to refer in particular to meals with ritual significance.

**Shabbat** (Hebrew; in Yiddish, Shabbes, Shabbos) The weekly day of rest beginning Friday at sunset and ending Saturday at nightfall, ushered in by the lighting of candles on Friday evening and the recitation of blessings over wine and challah (egg bread); a day of celebration as well as prayer, on which it is customary to eat three festive meals, attend synagogue services and refrain from doing any work or travelling.

**Shavuot** (Hebrew; literally, weeks) A two-day Jewish holiday that occurs seven weeks after Pesach. The holiday commemorates both God giving the Torah to the Jewish people on Mount Sinai and the wheat harvest in the land of Israel.

**Shoah** (Hebrew; literally, catastrophe) A term used since the 1940s to refer to the Holocaust.

**shochet** (Hebrew; in Yiddish, *shoyket*) Ritual slaughterer. A man conversant with the religious teaching of *kashruth*, trained to slaughter animals according to Jewish law and to check that the product meets the various criteria of kosher slaughter.

**SS** (abbreviation of Schutzstaffel; Defence Corps) The SS was established in 1925 as Adolf Hitler's elite corps of personal bodyguards. Under the direction of Heinrich Himmler, its membership grew from 280 in 1929 to 50,000 when the Nazis came to power in 1933, and to nearly a quarter of a million on the eve of World War II. The SS was comprised of the Allgemeine-SS (General SS) and the Waffen-SS (Armed, or Combat SS). The General SS dealt with policing and the enforcement of Nazi racial policies in Germany and the Nazi-occupied countries. An important unit within the SS was the Reichssicherheitshauptamt (RSHA, the Central Office of Reich Security), whose responsibility included the Gestapo (Geheime Staatspolizei). The SS ran the concentration and death camps, with all their associated economic enterprises, and also fielded its own Waffen-SS military divisions, including some recruited from the occupied countries.

**Tisha B'Av** (Hebrew; literally, ninth day of the month of Av) A Jewish day that commemorates tragedies that have befallen the Jewish people, especially the destruction of the two Holy Temples in Jerusalem; the First Temple was burned by the Babylonians in 423 BCE, and the Second Temple was destroyed by the Romans in 70 CE. The day is recognized through a twenty-five-hour fast.

**Treaty of Trianon** One of the five treaties produced at the 1919 Paris Peace Conference organized by the victors of World War I. The Treaty of Trianon imposed a harsh peace on Hungary, exacting reparations and redrawing its borders so that Hungary lost over two-thirds of its territory and about two-thirds of its inhabitants.

*Tsena u'Rena* (Yiddish; Come Out and See) The first major original work to be written in Yiddish for women. Compiled in the early 1600s, it was a collection of traditional biblical commentary and folklore tied to the weekly Torah readings.

*tzedakah* (charity; from the Hebrew word *tzadik*; righteousness) The act of charity, an important concept in Judaism.

**United Nations Relief and Rehabilitation Administration** (UNRRA) An international relief agency created at a 44-nation conference in Washington, DC, on November 9, 1943, to provide economic assistance and basic necessities to war refugees. It was especially active in repatriating and assisting refugees in the formerly Nazi-occupied European nations immediately after World War II.

**Wehrmacht** (German) The German army during the Third Reich.

**Women's International Zionist Organization** (WIZO) An organization founded in England in 1920 to help women and children in what was then British Mandate Palestine and is now Israel. WIZO is currently the largest women's Zionist organization in the world.

**yellow Star of David** (in Yiddish, *geleh lateh,* yellow patch) The six-pointed Star of David (in Hebrew, Magen David) that is the ancient and most recognizable symbol of Judaism. During World War II, Jews in Nazi-occupied areas were frequently forced to wear a badge or armband with the Star of David on it as an identifying mark of their lesser status and to single them out as targets for persecution.

**yeshiva** (Hebrew) A Jewish educational institution in which religious texts such as the Torah and Talmud are studied.

**yeshiva *bochurs*** (Hebrew) *Bochurs* refers to young unmarried males; yeshiva *bochurs* are young male yeshiva students. *See also* yeshiva.

**Zionism** A movement promoted by the Viennese Jewish journalist Theodor Herzl, who argued in his 1896 book *Der Judenstaat* (The Jewish State) that the best way to resolve the problem of antisemitism and persecution of Jews in Europe was to create an independent Jewish state in the historic Jewish homeland of Biblical Israel. Zionists also promoted the revival of Hebrew as a Jewish national language.

Photographs

Judith's maternal grandparents, Aryeh Leib and Feige Leah Hofstadter.
Mezőkövesd, Hungary, circa 1940.

1  Judith's maternal grandfather and his sons. Back row, left to right: uncles Moshe
   and Zev. Front row, left to right: uncle Yaakov, grandfather Aryeh Leib Hofstadter
   and uncle Heszu. Mezőkövesd, Hungary, circa 1935.

2  Judith's mother, Rachel Schwarcz, on the far left, and Judith's great-aunts.
   Mezőkövesd, Hungary, circa 1935.

Judith (right) and her cousin Rose Weisz. Ujhely, Hungary, circa 1938.

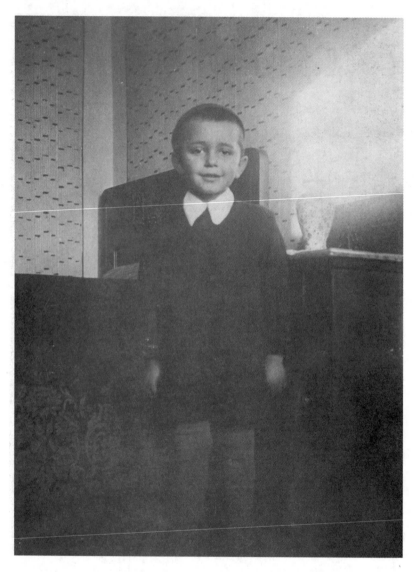

Judith's brother Menachem, five years old. Szerencs, Hungary, circa 1943.

1 Judith soon after liberation with her nine Lager sisters (camp sisters), who had worked together at Auschwitz. Judith sewed all the outfits herself out of Nazi officer bedsheets. Top row, from left to right: Greta, Selma, Klara, Magda and Judith. Bottom row, from left to right: Judith's cousin Regina Hofstadter, Bracha, Anika, Taubie and Margit. Schwerin, Germany, spring 1945.

2 Judith. Italy, fall 1946.

1 Judith in post-liberation Europe, circa 1945.
2 Judith and her husband-to-be, Béla Rubinstein. Grugliasco, Italy. May 1946.
3 Judith's sister-in-law Vera Rubinstein (left) and Judith. Grugliasco, Italy, circa 1946.
4 Judith and Béla on their wedding day. Grugliasco, Italy. June 9, 1947.

1   Judith and Béla's wedding day in the DP camp. Judith is in a white dress sitting
    in the second row and Béla is next to her. Cousins Magda and Béla Zimmerman
    are on their left; Vera Rubinstein is on their right; and Judith's husband's brother
    Armin Rubinstein is behind Judith. Grugliasco, Italy. June 9, 1947.

2   Left to right: Judith's husband's brother Armin Rubinstein; Judith and her
    husband, Béla; Béla's niece Magda Zimmerman with her son, David, and her hus-
    band, Béla; Vera and her husband, Dezső Rubinstein; Béla's niece Kicsi and her
    husband, Judith's cousin Sandor Hofstadter. UNRRA DP camp #17, Grugliasco,
    Italy. 1947.

1  Judith's brother Yitzhak Schwarcz. France, circa 1948.
2  Béla's brother Armin Rubinstein, Judith and Béla. Grugliasco, Italy, 1948.
3  Judith and her son, Eli. Grugliasco, Italy. Summer 1948.
4  Judith and Béla. Toronto, winter 1949.

1 In the back, from left to right: Judith's husband's brother Dezső Rubinstein, cousin Sandor Hofstadter and husband, Béla Rubinstein, behind their wives. Middle row: Vera Rubinstein, Kicsi Hofstadter and Judith. Front: Dezső and Vera's daughter, Annie; Sandor and Kicsi's son, George; Béla and Judith's son, Eli. Toronto, 1952.

2 Wedding of Judith's cousin Imre and Sophie Hofstadter. Back row, left to right: cousins Vili (Zev) Hofstadter and Kicsi Hofstadter, great-uncle Heszu Hofstadter and Elsa Hofstadter. Front row: Judith's husband, Béla, Judith with her son, Eli, Judith's cousins Sophie and Imre Hofstadter, Judith's husband's brother Dezső Rubinstein and his wife, Vera, Judith's great-aunt Rozsi Hofstadter and Willy and Manci Wohlburg. Toronto, 1951.

Judith and her son, Eli, at Sunnyside Beach in Toronto, circa 1952.

Judith and Béla with their children, Rochelle and Eli. Toronto, summer 1955.

1   On the left: Vera Rubinstein with her two daughters, Susie and Annie. In the middle: Kicsi Hofstadter with her son George on her shoulders and son Tommy in front. On the right: Judith with her son, Eli, behind her and daughter, Rochelle, in front. Toronto, summer 1955.

2   Judith and Béla with their daughter, Rochelle, at three years old. Toronto, August 1956.

Judith's daughter, Rochelle; husband, Béla; son, Eli; and Judith at Eli's bar mitz-vah. Toronto, March 1961.

1   Judith and her brother Yitzhak Schwarcz. Niagara Falls, Ontario. August 1974.
2   Judith's daughter, Rochelle, Judith and Rochelle's son, Jesse. Visiting the Jewish cemetery in Mezőkövesd, Hungary. 1983.

1

2

1 Judith and Béla with their granddaughter Tamar Rubinstein. Toronto, 1978.
2 Judith and Béla with their grandson Zekiel G. Rubinstein Kaplan. Toronto, 1987.

In the back, left to right: Judith's granddaughter Tamar; son, Eli; daughter-in-law, Renée; grandson Ilan; daughter, Rochelle; granddaughter Alisha Rubinstein Kaplan; son-in-law, Allan. In the middle: Judith and Béla. In the front, left to right: grandchildren Jesse Armin Rubinstein Kaplan, Zekiel G. Rubinstein Kaplan and Hadassa and Erez Rubinstein. Grandson Ilan's bar mitzvah. Toronto, September 1990.

Judith at her grandson Jesse Armin Rubinstein Kaplan's wedding. Toronto, May 24, 2009.

1 Judith at Rochelle's farm in Hillsburgh, Ontario, northwest of Toronto. Circa 2011.
2 A gathering of four generations: Judith, her great-grandson Charlie Kaplan, her daughter, Rochelle, and her grandson Jesse Armin Rubinstein Kaplan. Toronto, 2012.

# Index

The Azrieli Foundation was established in 1989 to realize and extend the philanthropic vision of David J. Azrieli, C.M., C.Q., M.Arch. The Foundation's mission is to support a wide spectrum of initiatives in education and research. The Azrieli Foundation is an active supporter of programs in the fields of education, the education of architects, scientific and medical research, and the arts. The Azrieli Foundation's many initiatives include: the Holocaust Survivor Memoirs Program, which collects, preserves, publishes and distributes the written memoirs of survivors in Canada; the Azrieli Institute for Educational Empowerment, an innovative program successfully working to keep at-risk youth in school; the Azrieli Fellows Program, which promotes academic excellence and leadership on the graduate level at Israeli universities; the Azrieli Music Project, which celebrates and fosters the creation of high-quality new Jewish orchestral music; and the Azrieli Neurodevelopmental Research Program, which supports advanced research on neurodevelopmental disorders, particularly Fragile X and Autism Spectrum Disorders.